The National Portrait Gallery of Kessa

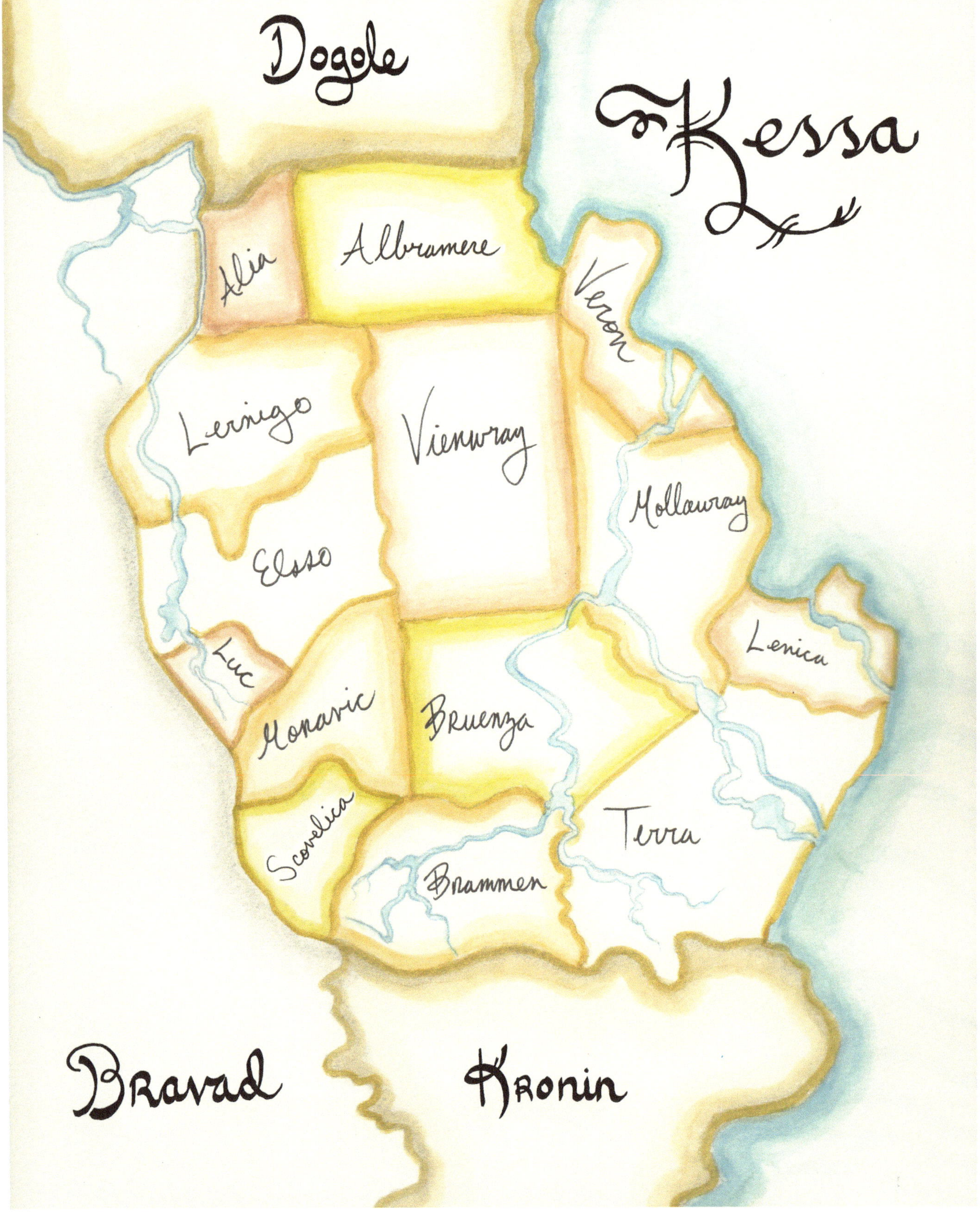
Dogole
Kessa
Alia
Albramere
Veron
Lernigo
Vienwray
Mollawray
Elsso
Lenica
Luc
Monavic
Bruenza
Terra
Scovelica
Brammen
Bravad
Kronin

The National Portrait Gallery of Kessa

The Art of Arabella Proffer

COOPERATIVE PRESS
Cleveland, Ohio

ISBN 13: 978-1937513023
First Edition, revised
Published by Cooperative Press
www.cooperativepress.com

Cooperative Press
info@cooperativepress.com
or 13000 Athens Ave C288, Lakewood, OH 44107 USA

For Cooperative Press:
Senior editor: Shannon Okey

Thank You

My husband Ben; Shannon Okey & Tamas Jakab; Veronica & Keith Harrison; Mom & Ross; Mary Ann & Roman Szporluk; my brothers Ian, Chris, and Andrew; David Miretsky, Suzi Becker; Lee Joseph; Dana Depew; William Rupnik Gallery; Art Whino Gallery; Parlor Gallery; The Velvet Tango Room; Cathie Bleck; Michelle Muldrow; Madeleine Monyleaux; Scott G. Brooks; Tara McPherson; Josh Geiser; Molly Crabapple; Mary Urbas; Susan Danko; Dott Schneider; Helen Schneider; Kathleen & George Nemeth; Brendan Mullen (RIP); Johnny Carlyon (RIP); well-wishers; enemies; and fans.

Contents

Noble Families of Kessa: A Selection

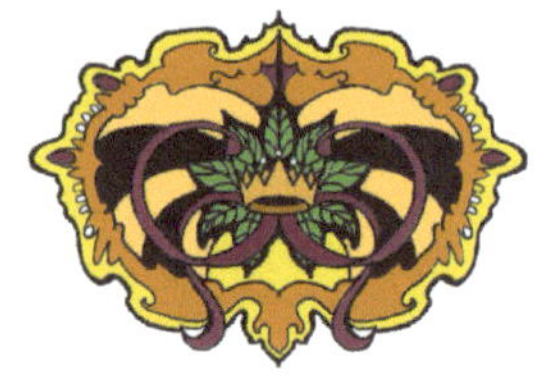

Thad the Black = Alexeevna

Lord Matias of Moravic **Baron Malachi of Moravic** = **Alexandria of Lenica, Baroness of Moravic** ***Belanna of Bravad**

***Lady Penelope** = Lord Jules

Baron Luca of Moravic = Elizabetta of Brammen

Einar, 1st Marquess of Moravic **Elizabetta the 2nd** = Lord Chamberlaine Henrik

Kristoff, 2nd Earl Vero Catherine Lanya Varya **Elizabetta the 3rd** = Dmitri, Marquess of Elsso

Baron Rudolfo of Lernigo = Lady Katya **Franz, Earl of Elsso** = **Annabel of Alia**

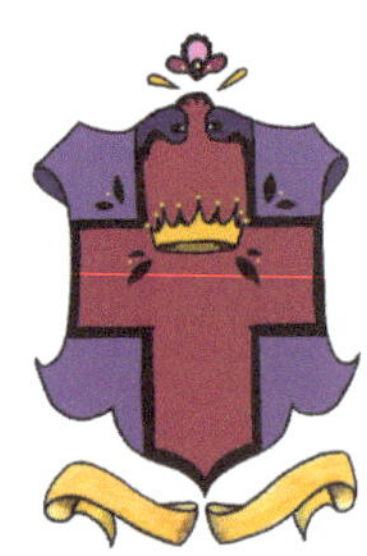

Lord Leo of Brammen = **Lady Lucrezia of Terra**

Lord Ebbot Lionel Marco Lady Sasha = Baron Andre of Luc

Alexia de Luc = **Simon, 1st Earl of Luc**

Vlad, 2nd Earl of Luc = **Nayanna of Alia, Countess of Luc**

Misha, 3rd Earl of Luc = **Dinara of Terra**

Misha the 2nd, 4th Earl of Luc Lord Mikel Lady Arya **Violante, Duchess of Mollawray** = Henri, Duke of Mollawray

Augustus, Earl of Veron = **Countess Christabelle** ***Lady Justine** **Lexia, Marquise of Vienwray** = **Adolphus, Marquess of Vienwray**

Theodora of Terra = Heinrik, Earl of Elsso

Charlotte of Bravad = **Alexi, Marquess of Terra** Varya 3 sons

Lord Basil = **Lady Fulvia of Terra** Lady Lenor

Laszlo, Duke of Scovelica = **Varuca, Duchess of Scovelica** Lady Nigella

Claude, Duke of Bruenza = **Beatrice, Duchess of Bruenza** **Lady Evangeline**

Lady Eugenia = Lord Cecil Lord Armand = **Lady Alexis of Veron**

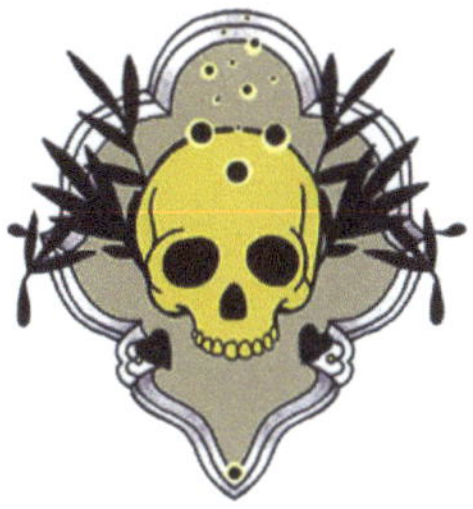

Count Lucas of Albramere = **Countess Jaecine of Albramere**

Latis, Earl of Vienwray = **Lady Christina of Albramere** **Lady Marcella** Lady Gianna

Lord Frederick of Vienwray = Lady Maria of Dogole Jacob, 2nd Earl of Vienwray

Baron Rudolfo, Viscount of Vienwray = *** Margaret** **Ingrid** Lady Kitty Hart Lord Mayor George 9 others

Friederica of Vienwray = Maxim, 4th Duke of Lernigo

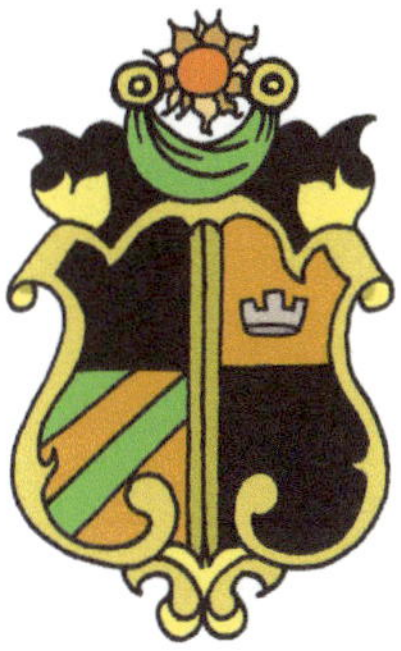

* *indicates illegitimate or dubious origin*
indicates portrait in this book

FOREWORD

Quite often when I should have been studying, for whatever major I'd chosen that semester, I would spend that precious time looking at art instead. The contemporary artists I was learning about were creating new worlds, dripping with imagination and pop culture references. While these worlds provided a good escape from the day to day monotony where many people—including myself—seemed stuck, they rarely contained elements that could be linked to my own personality and the subcultures I grew up in. Sure there were monsters, pin-up girls, and science fiction imagery, but rarely would I see a character that reminded me of the personalities that helped shape me into what I am today.

Around the time that I created my first art site, I switched majors to art history and began to research contemporary art at a feverish pace. One of the first artists I met was Arabella Proffer, and she has been one of the few people with whom I have kept in constant contact. What first drew me into her work was the fact it contained characters I knew and grew up with. Rebellious kids with piercings, shaved heads, mohawks, tattoos, and clothing as loud as we were. Arabella herself was into the punk culture, but also grew up surrounded by the art of Sergei Soudeikine and David Miretsky. She eventually went to the California Institute of Arts for a BFA in fine art while learning animation; studying under artists such as under John Mandel, Derek Boshier, Jules Engel, as well as Richard Wright. While Arabella no longer sports a leather jacket adorned with spikes, or a bleached mohawk, the influence of her surroundings vibrates throughout her work as clear as the influence Tamara de Lempicka or Christian Schad has had in the styling of it.

No matter how much resistance is put on any subculture, the strongest ones are soon assimilated and become pop culture, or at least a water-downed version of it. Living in a city as intense as San Francisco, you see how many subcultures there are, but how many of them have been fully realized in the mind of one person, such as what Arabella has done? Not only do these fictional aristocrats have names, but demeanors and personalities that radiate from their visages and adornments. Each character is attached to maps, crests, and family trees. Looking at these portraits you are peering into an entire world, one that is as perfectly at home in oils as it would be in a book or movie. Each one of these paintings is a perfect blend of Mannerist ideals, classical painting techniques, decadence, and heritage. These paintings are the Daguerreotypes or Cabinet Photos that were once passed down through the generations. In this world the punks and goths are the upper class, and those with the most wealth and power are clearly made evident in their costumes and hair color. What successfully brings this world to life is Arabella's passion for storytelling, the great lengths she goes to research costumes, to understand the codes of European nobility, and the skill at which she renders the figures. Each painting is another life she brought into existence; imagine this book as it should be, the antiquarian tome these families would pass down to future generations.

—Josh Geiser

Geiser is a San Francisco-based designer, curator, art historian of the pop surrealist movement, founder of art site CreepMachine (creepmachine.com). He works for the Contemporary Jewish Museum.

PRIVATE EMPIRE

This series brings together my interests in decadence, rich paintings, and ancestor worship. I've always enjoyed exploring the particular roles that beauty, vanity, entitlement and virtue play in shaping aesthetic outcomes. Fashion, an outreach of beauty and vanity, figures in my work as a declaration of power and self-confidence, especially the styles of punk and other subgenres with their musical stance and anti-establishment tendencies. What was once considered counter-culture or unique is now so widely accepted that the effect of these appearances superimposed on traditional ones has always been of interest. To me, the stylings of punk and goth manage to be both rebellious and regal.

My work is concerned with identity and history; ideas and representations of counter-culture paired with tradition. I wondered punk or gothic styles might be adopted by aristocrats and social elites if it were part of their own decoration for serious portraits; ones that would be left as a reminder of their legacy. Traditionally, each portrait preserves what may later be a historical moment. In the case of this series however, the "historical" moments are of my own imagination. Between the peerage and costume research, I like to combine aristocratic traditions and names that draw from Slavic, Latin, and Anglo-Saxon origins – and while the people, places, and biographies are all made up, it lends authenticity in a surreal way.

I began this series in late 2000, perhaps as a way of creating fake ancestors for myself. As an American, I always found the world of the aristocracy – of codes, and class, and rank – fascinating, because it is a system that Americans wanted done away with, a system that is now near extinction. I found it so amazing that there were people and places in Europe that possessed relics of the past that were so beautiful, lovingly crafted, and so much more interesting than a photograph because they record both truth and fantasy.

The more portraits I have created, the more my little empire has grown; adding new stories, characters, and family members. It is a mild obsession that shows no sign of slowing down. I'm mildly obsessed with ancient refinement, eccentricity and privileged culture – all mingled with a hint of joy and the bizarre. Part of the experience for the viewer is to interact with these characters, imagine what they were like, and maybe, even recognize hints of his or her self.

– Arabella Proffer

Alexandria of Lenica, Baroness of Moravic (1540–1599)

Illegitimate great-granddaughter of King Vlad the III. Wealthy, with powerful ancestors and a prime commodity; her parents were ready to offer her like a sacrificial pawn to any dubious royal game that was afoot – so she would become queen, legitimately. She was happy to settle for lesser aristocrat. After meeting Baron Malachi at a foxhunt, they were married secretly before slipping away to his home in Moravic.

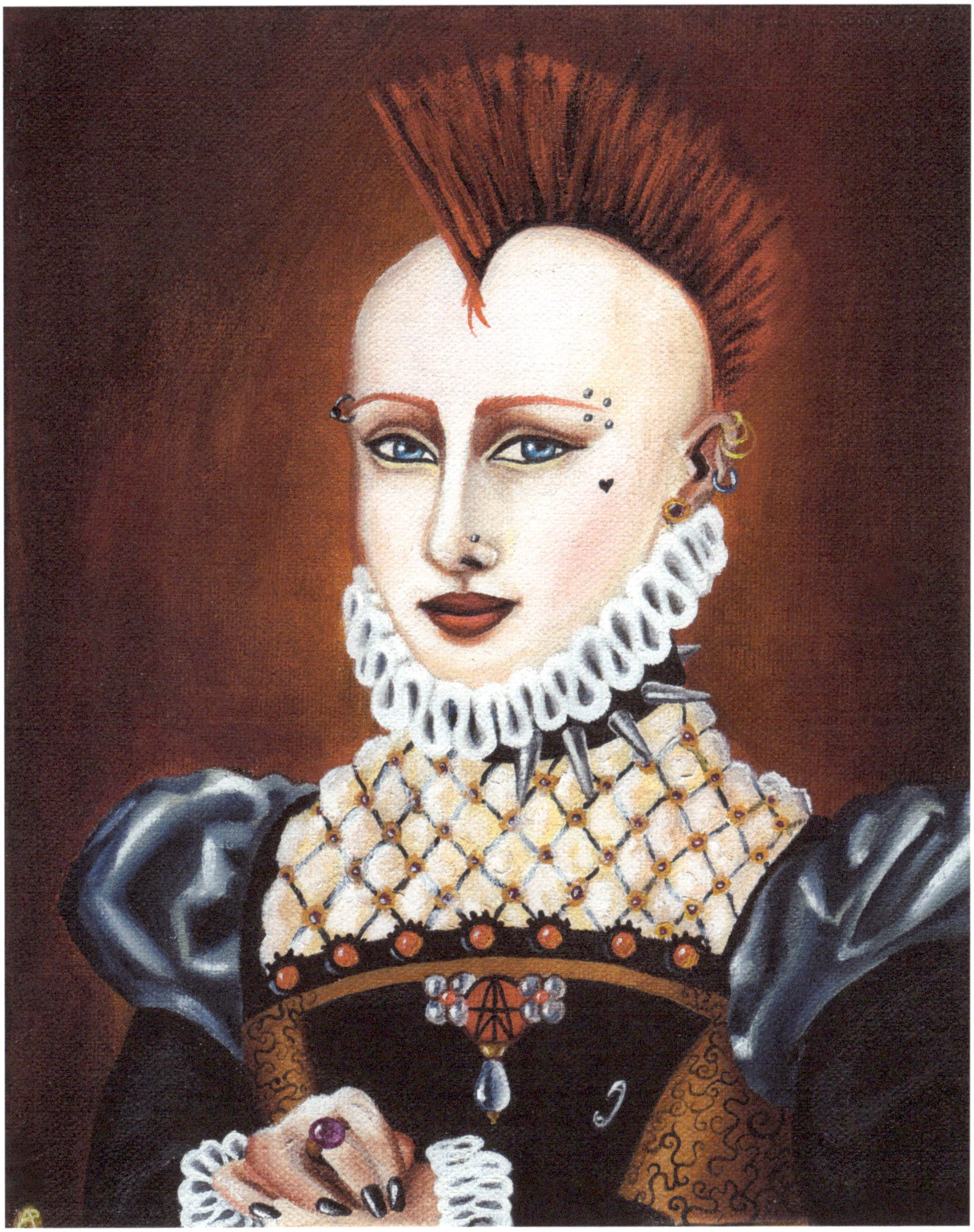

8 x 10" OIL ON CANVAS

Baron Malachi of Moravic (1528–1600)

First son to Thad the Black of Kronin. After his father defected from Kronin and settled the family in Moravic, Malachi was given the title Baron, for engineering the farm irrigation systems and increasing the agricultural production in his county. He was part of the new wave of men who were self-made, and looked on with suspicion by the nobility for not being of ancient lineage. He married Lady Alexandria of Lenica in 1559.

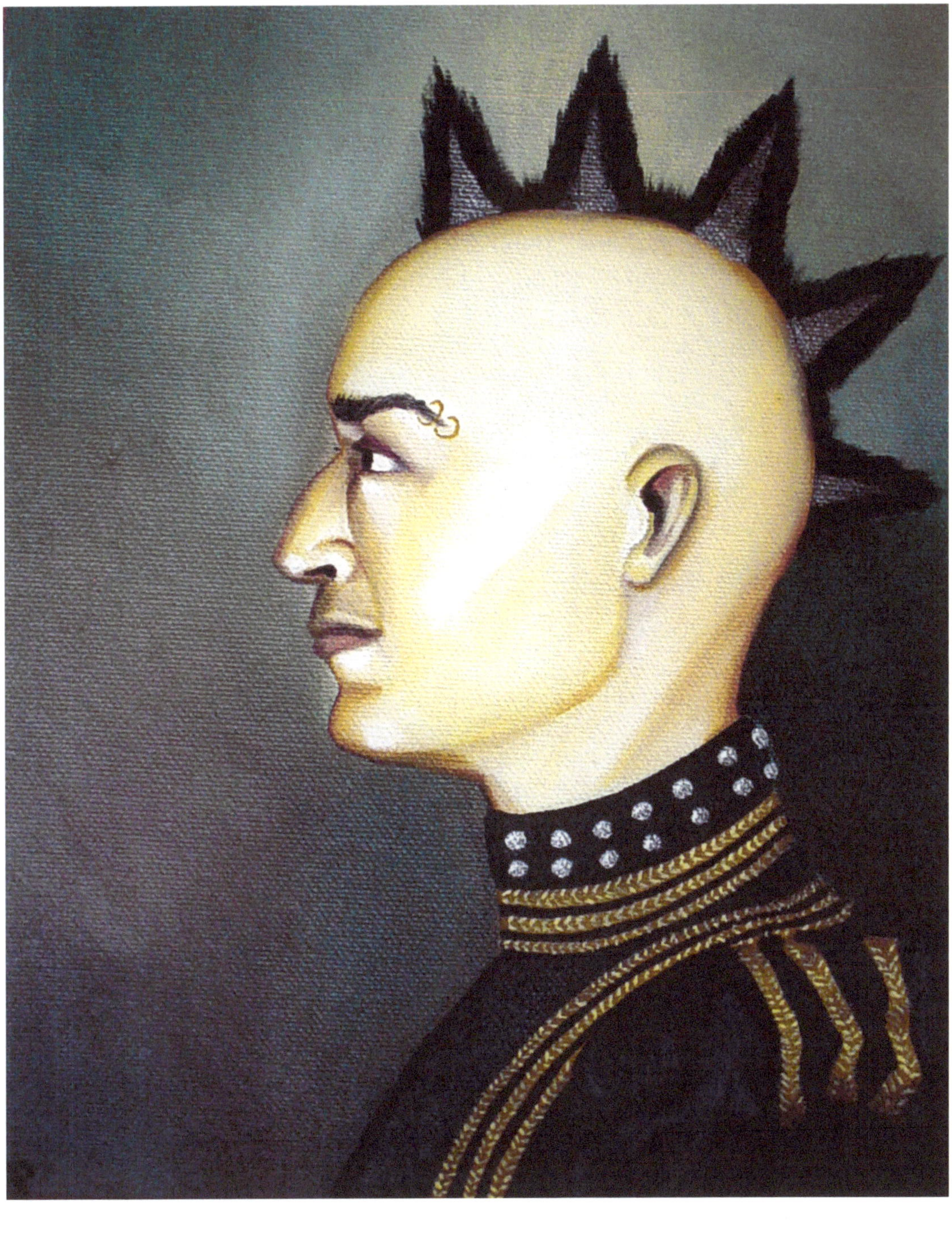

8 x 10" oil on canvas

Lord Matias of Moravic (1530–1564)

Second son of Thad the Black. Lacking in the royal connections older brother had attained, and not being considered in league with the super-rich of the aristocracy, the loss of two wives to disease would spur him to become a celebrated poet and intellectual. He was killed in a riding accident, the same day his 12th book was published.

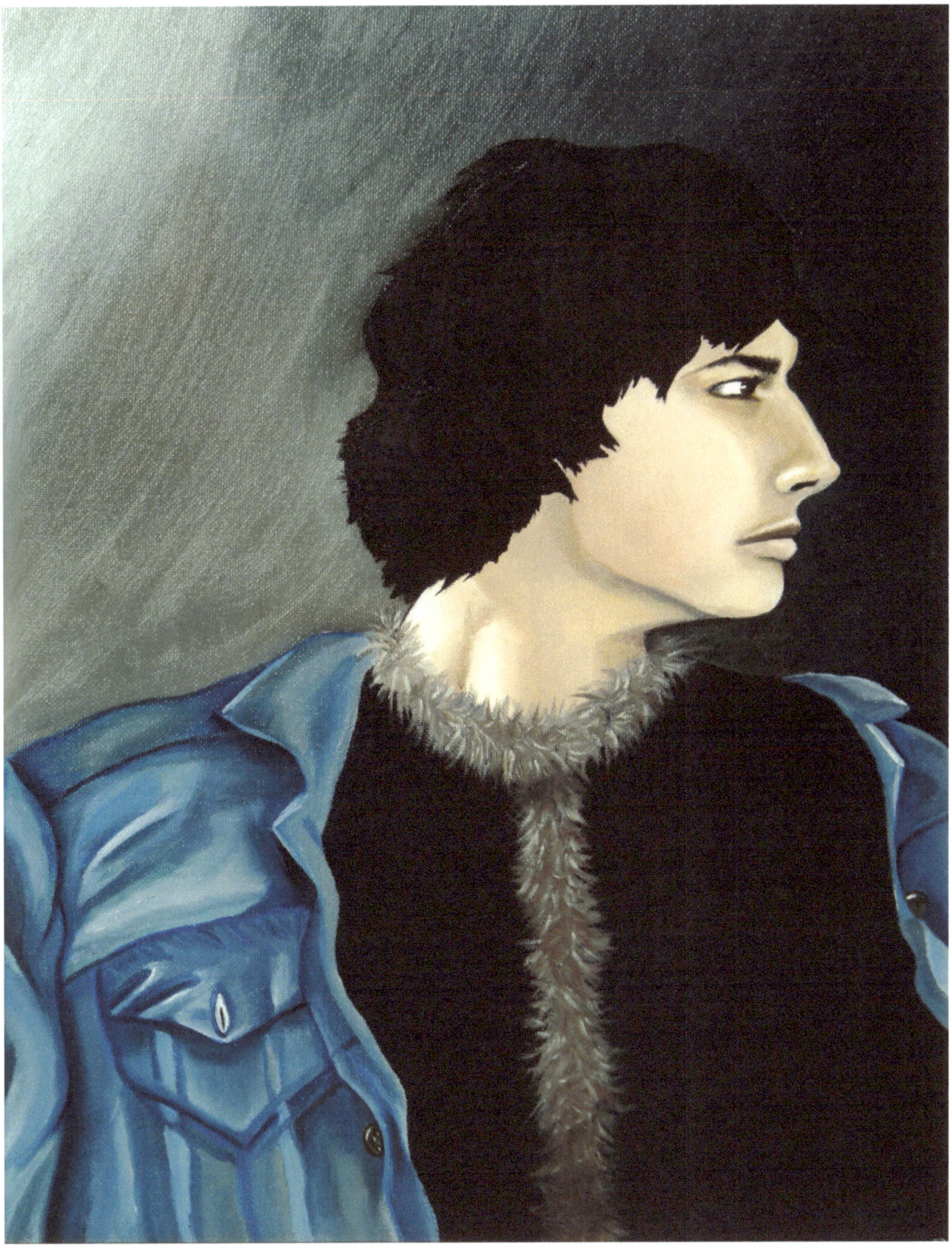

16 x 20" OIL ON CANVAS

Belanna of Bravad (1531–1589)

Though it is still not clear what her distant relation was to Baroness Alexandria, she was accepted into the court society circles and became confidant to many of the noble women despite the scandal surrounding her sister Lady Penelope. She was a great archer, known for her theme parties and followed for her fashion sense by young women. Though never married, she had no trouble maintaining a fabulous lifestyle thanks to many admirers.

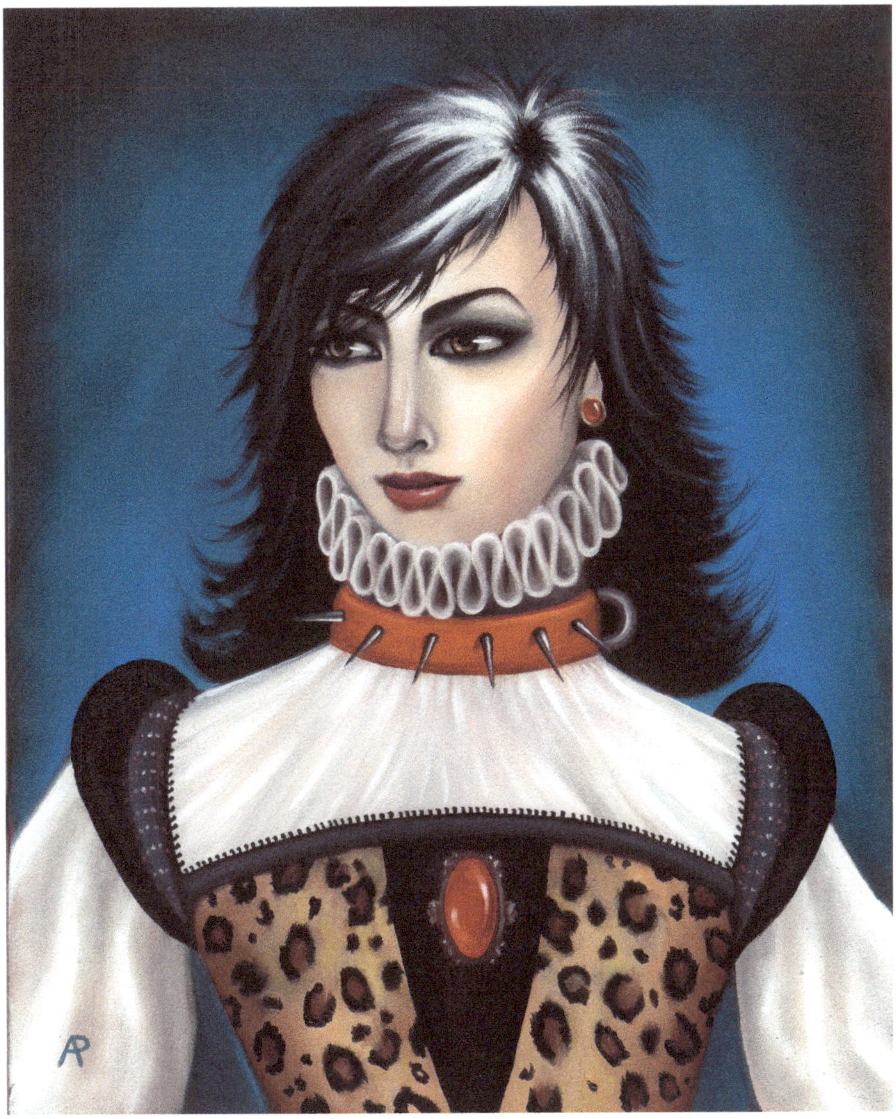

8 x 10" oil on panel

Lady Penelope
(1533–unknown)

Known for her charm, beauty, many affairs and illegitimate children, it was maintained she had once been a madam at a brothel where her two eldest daughters were employed. She also told everyone she was descended from a King. Despite being shunned in society at first, her powers and physical charms carried her until acquiring a title in marrying a newly created Baronet – thanks to her sister's connections. He mysteriously broke his neck after a fall down a marble staircase shortly after.

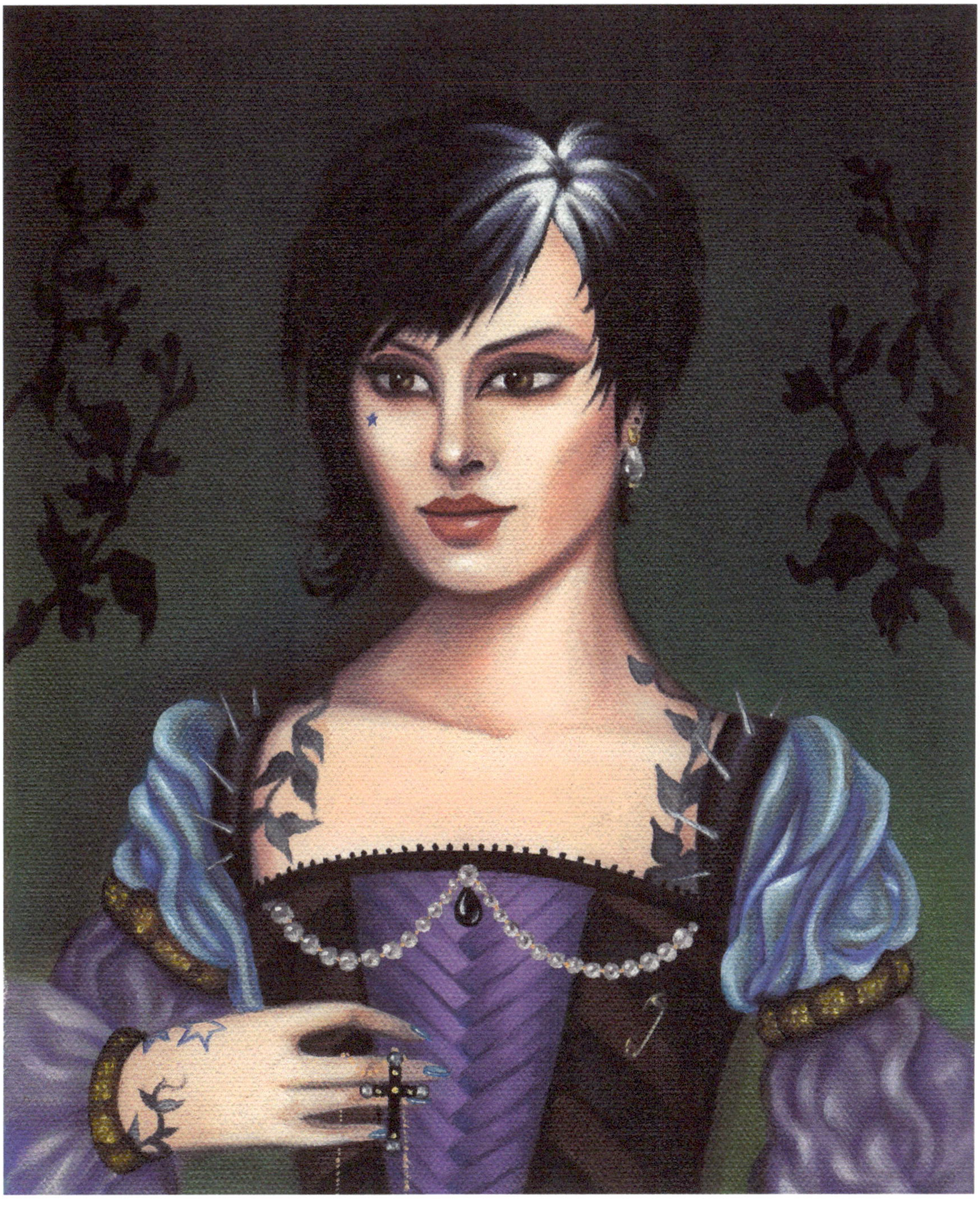

8 x 10" oil on canvas

Baron Luca and Baroness Elizabetta of Moravic (1556–1628)

Responsible for the construction of several forts along the border for Kessan military, as the family political powers and fortunes grew, so did their passion for collecting artwork. Renowned for the sculptures they acquired, the entire collection is still on display at the museum housed in their former residence, Tally Hall.

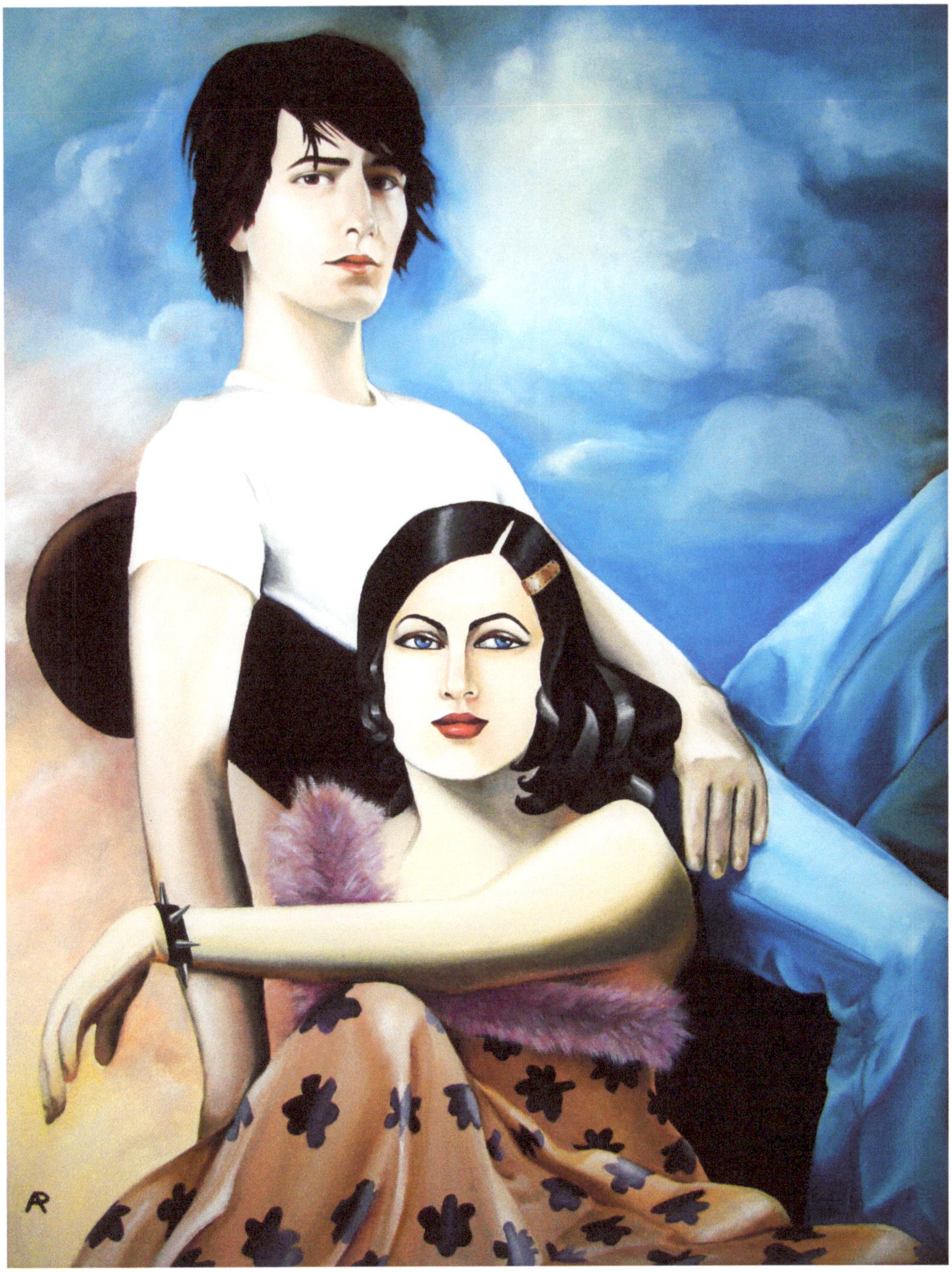

18 x 24" OIL ON CANVAS

Elizabetta the II (1580–1639)

After the death of her older brother, Einar, who was promoted to 1st Marquess of Moravic, her newly titled family line had seemed to be near extinction before it had begun. It fell unto Elizabetta to carry on their now affluent and demanding way of life by marrying above her. Her presentation at court paid off, in the form of Henrik, the Deputy and Lord Chamberlain who proposed days later. This was treated more as a business transaction than romantic gesture; Elizabetta was held in near captivity at Henrik's country estate with only her newly acquired and indomitable mother-in-law for company. Bound by rules, duty, and social codes that were still new to her, her mother-in-law set out to make the young lady worthy of her son's position. The tedious and often cruel 'lessons' her mother-in-law imposed helped Elizabetta to grow a thick skin and bloom into a grand dame in her own right. After 7 children (only 2 would survive into adulthood) she had become an exemplary Lady.

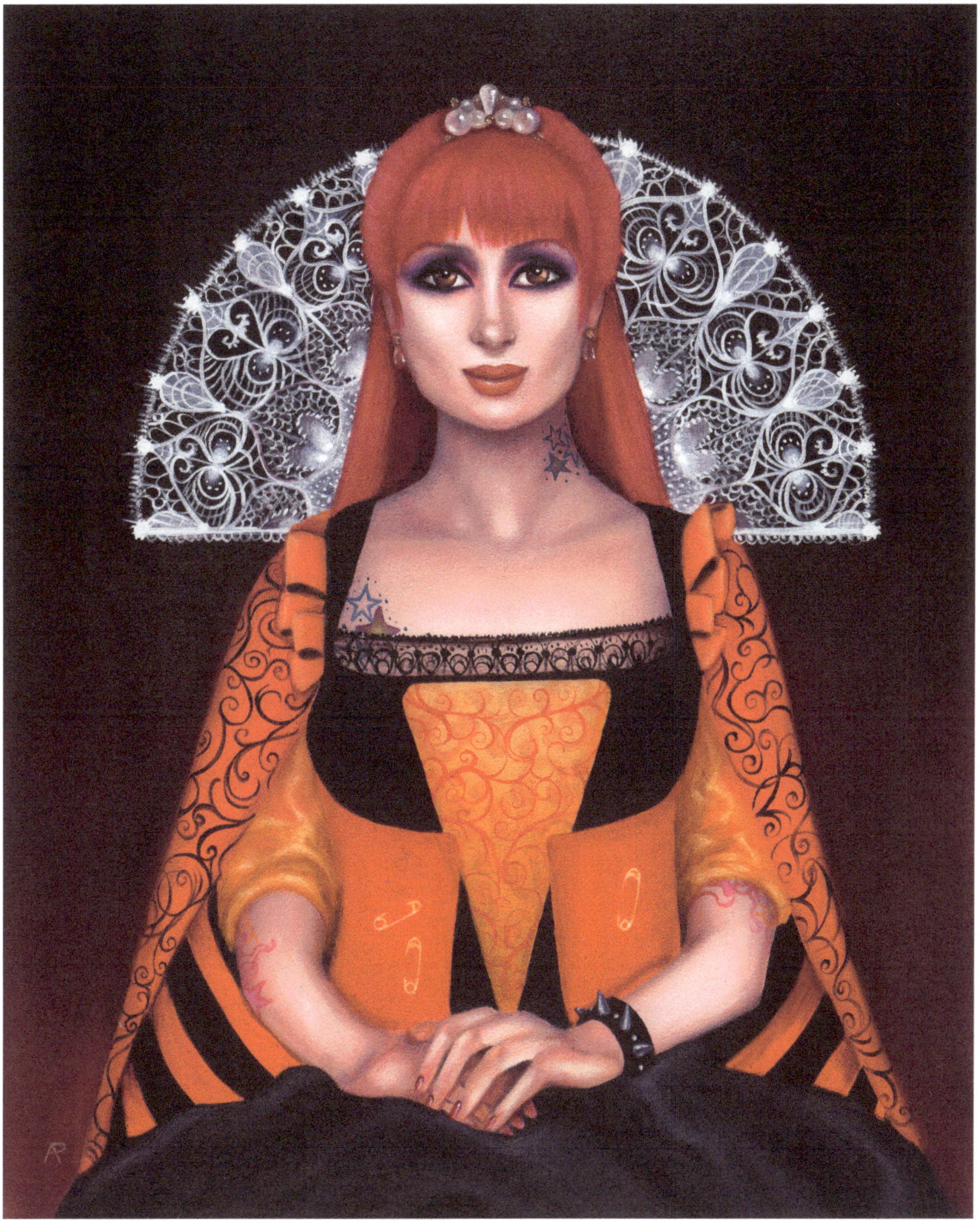

8 x 10" oil on panel

Elizabetta the III, Marquise of Elsso (1610–1679)

Granddaughter of Baron Luca & Elizabetta, she was an educated connoisseur of art, championship archer, and accomplished musician. After marrying the Marquess of Elsso, fortunes began to dwindle when her gambling brother became a regular visitor. She often used her jewelry to settle his debts; she was unaware that he was in fact winning, buying property and collecting rents throughout Kessa.

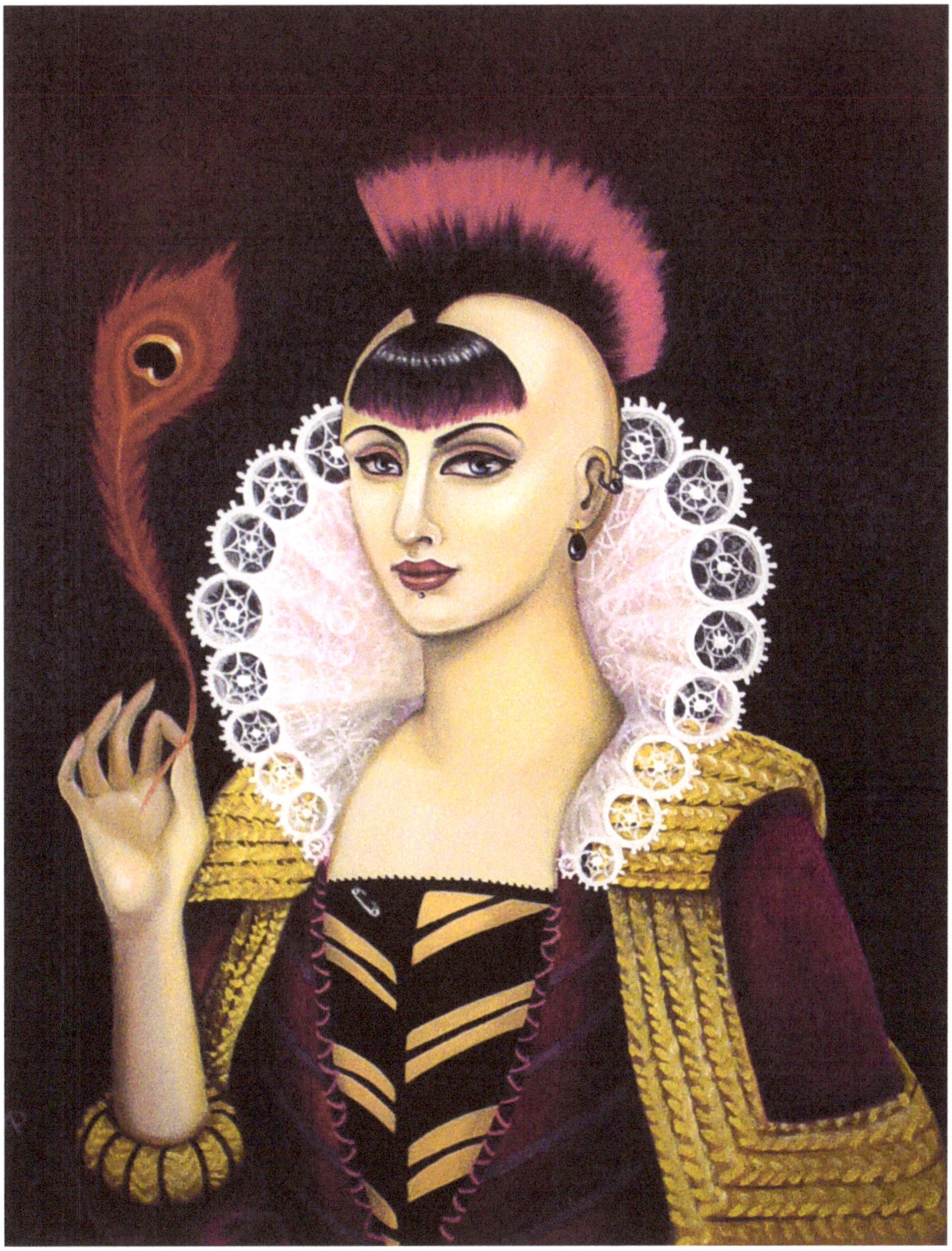

11 x 14" OIL ON PANEL

Annabel of Alia, Countess of Elsso (1656–1728)

To have been born in the county of Alia was not easy, known as "the land of tarts" as it was a popular starting point for ladies before moving to bigger and better brothels. Raised in a convent and given a proper debut by her parents, she still managed to lose her virginity to the Earl of Elsso in a broom closet – within the first hour of her debut ball. It was a splendid union; she was to be the emblem of class and sophistication within their social circles.

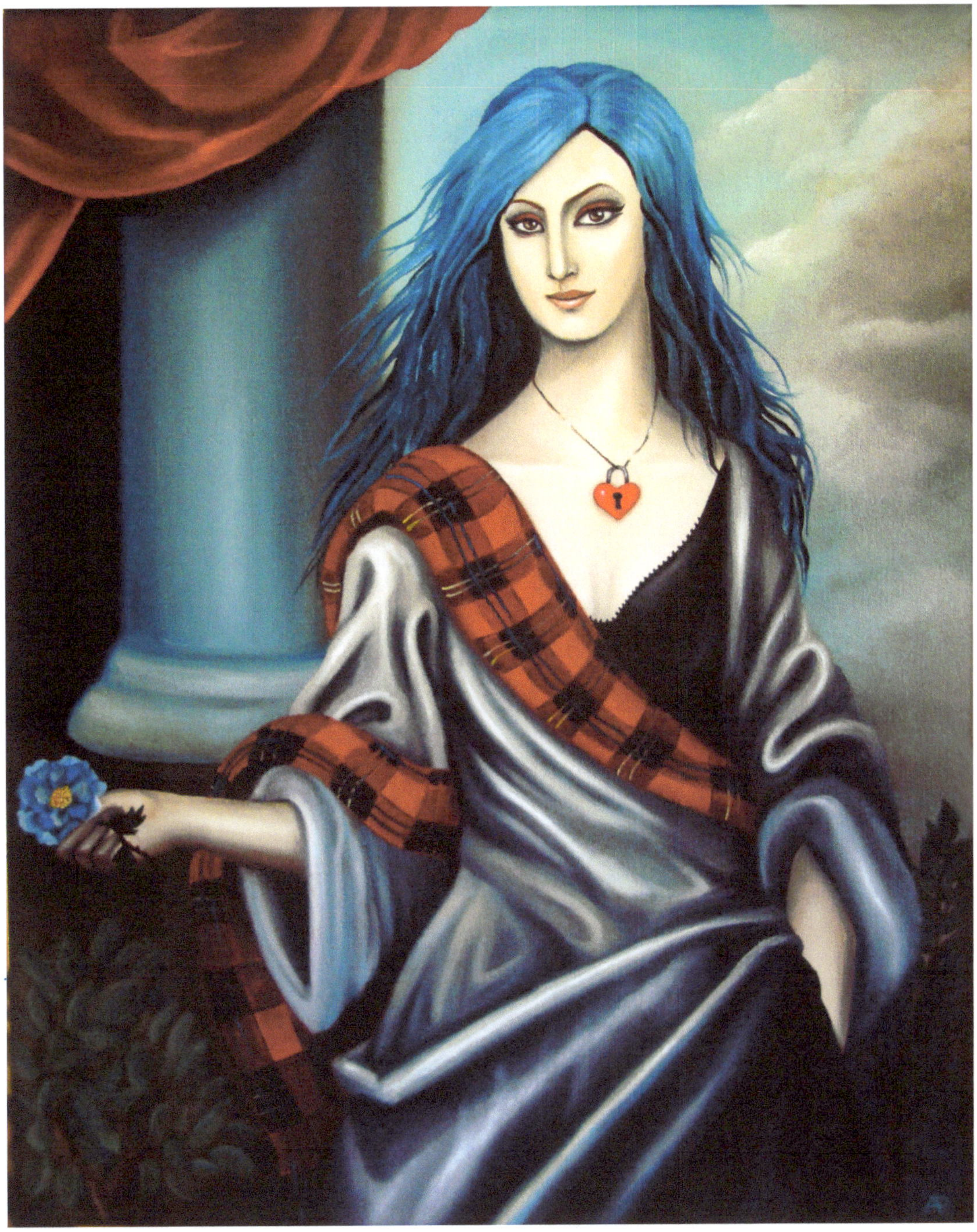

16 x 20" OIL ON CANVAS

Franz the Earl of Elsso (1654–1724)

Known as pleasant and forthright, it was after inheriting his gambling uncle's estates in several provinces that he became fascinated with the military and threw himself into writing about warfare and strategy, publishing thoughts and theories; all while conspicuously avoiding any active military duties. He would then abandon writing, finally attempting to assist with the battle of Kronin. Upon donning armor for the first time, he proclaimed it too heavy and was unable to walk more than 7 feet. It was then that he realized his writings never took into account the weight of armor and were utterly useless.

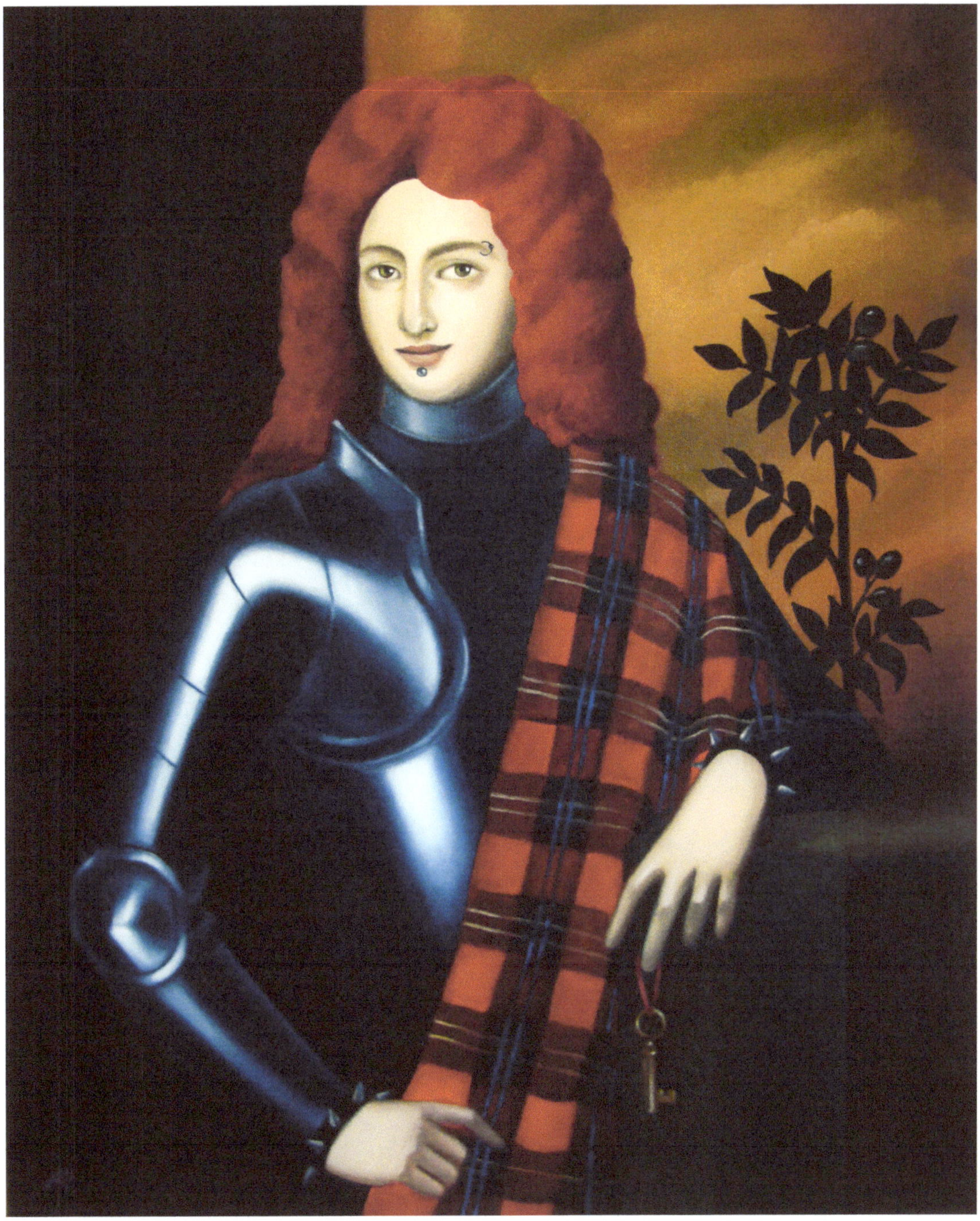

16 x 20" oil on canvas

Theodora the II (1442–1476)

After her husband was accidentally poisoned, she spent years traveling throughout the Middle East and Africa to meet witchdoctors and mystics, collecting their antidotes – paranoid of being poisoned as well. It is said the surge of leopard spots in aristocrat fashions had begun with her. She and four of her children later contracted malaria in eastern Africa – her oldest son the Marquess of Terra would be the only surviving family member.

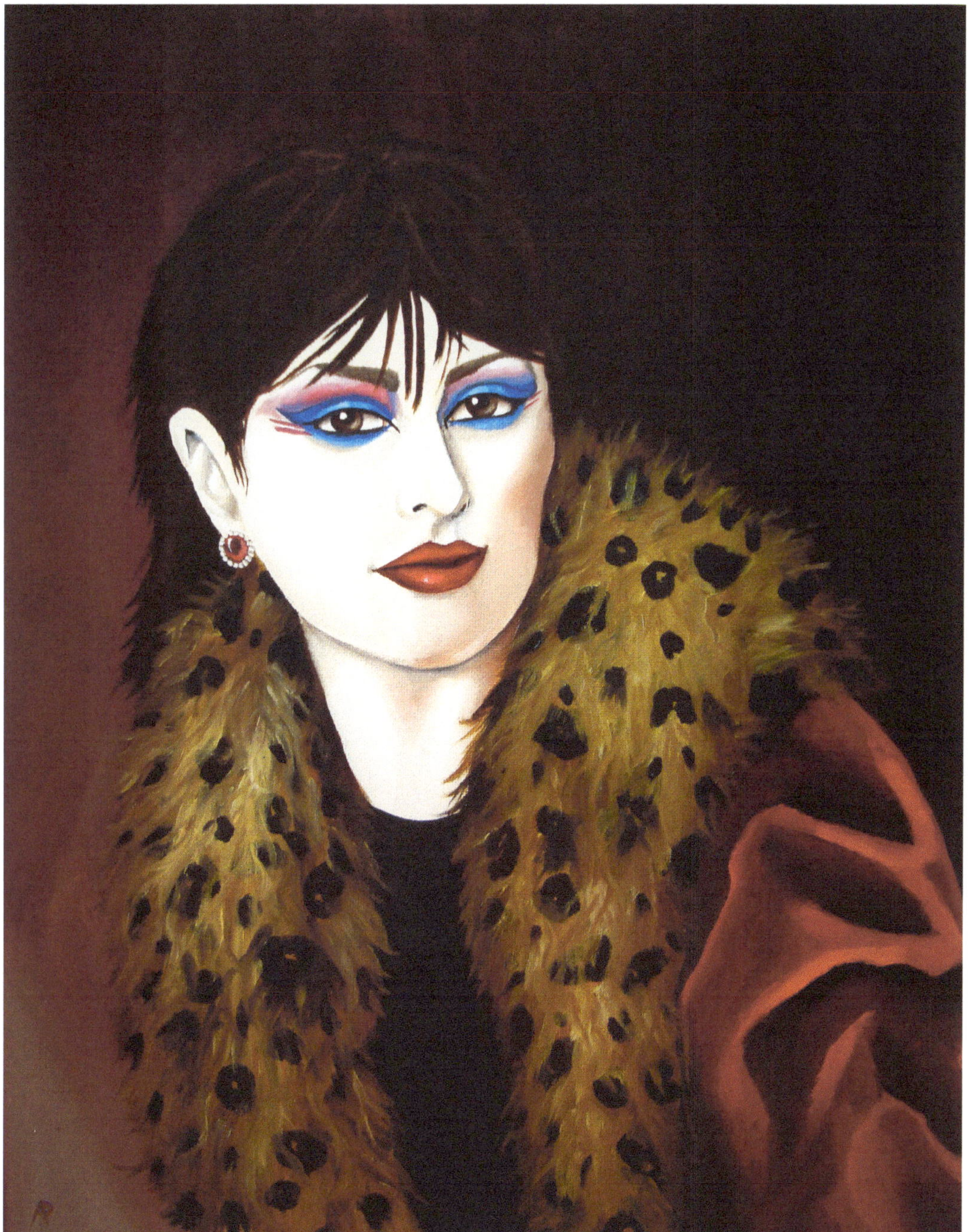

16 x 20" oil on canvas

Alexi, Marquess of Terra (1461–1589)

Despite family tragedy, his travels with his mother and meetings with medicine men had inspired a career importing, breeding and supplying royalty with his botanical creations. This would earn him an advanced title and eventually made him Kessa's first Master of the Horticulture. He married in 1486 to Charlotte of Bravad, whom it was rumored, was the orphan of a Mongolian warlord before her days raised in a convent. They would have five children.

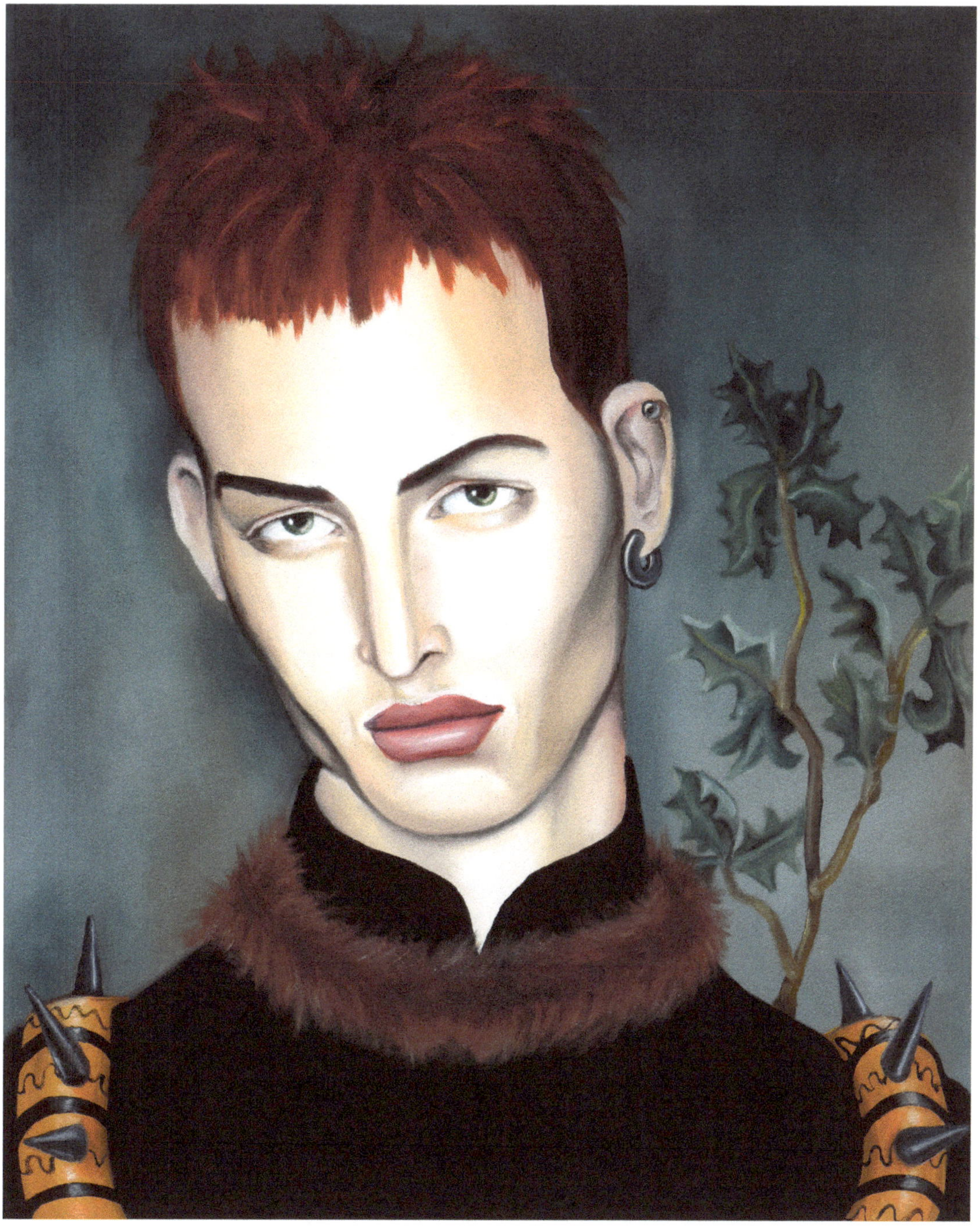

8 x 10" OIL ON PANEL

Lady Fulvia of Terra (1484–1511)

The youngest daughter of the Marquess of Terra, she was her father's favorite, always referred to as his "little joy". Betrothed to a Lord while still a child, her husband-to-be became smitten, thanks to a steady stream of portraits sent to him of the young girl as he waited for her to grow up. They were married when she was 15, and he was 33. After bearing two daughters, both Lord and Lady were killed in a horse carriage accident.

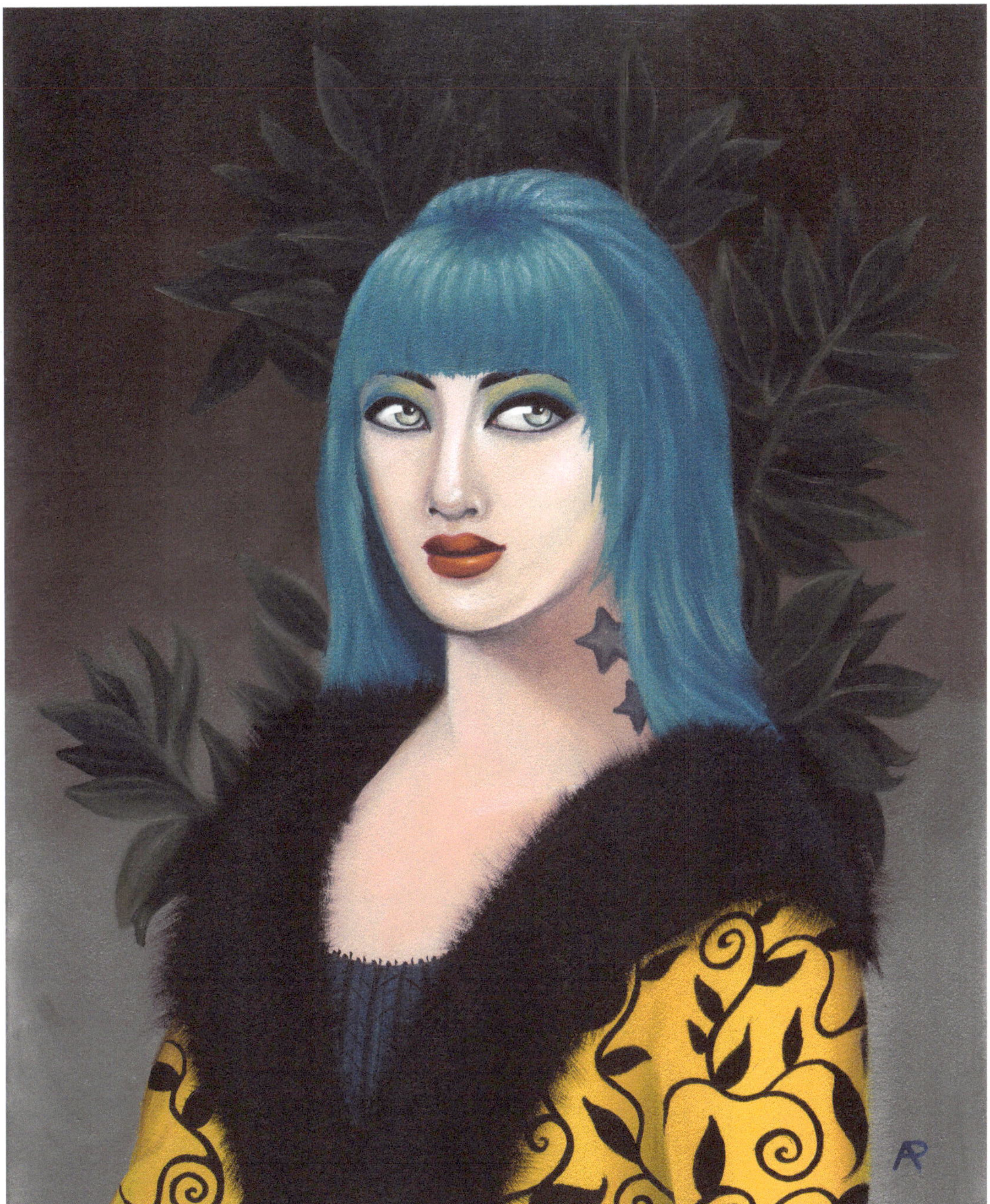

8 x 10" OIL ON PANEL

Varuca, Duchess of Scovelica (1512–1579)

First daughter to the 2nd Marquess of Terra. Married at the age of 14 to the Duke of Scovelica, her exotic looks and passion for horses made the rumors of her supposed Mongolian heredity popular within many social circles. Self-conscious about her height, she began wearing her hair in up in spikes as means to appear taller. This began a trend that would move in and out of fashion, for centuries.

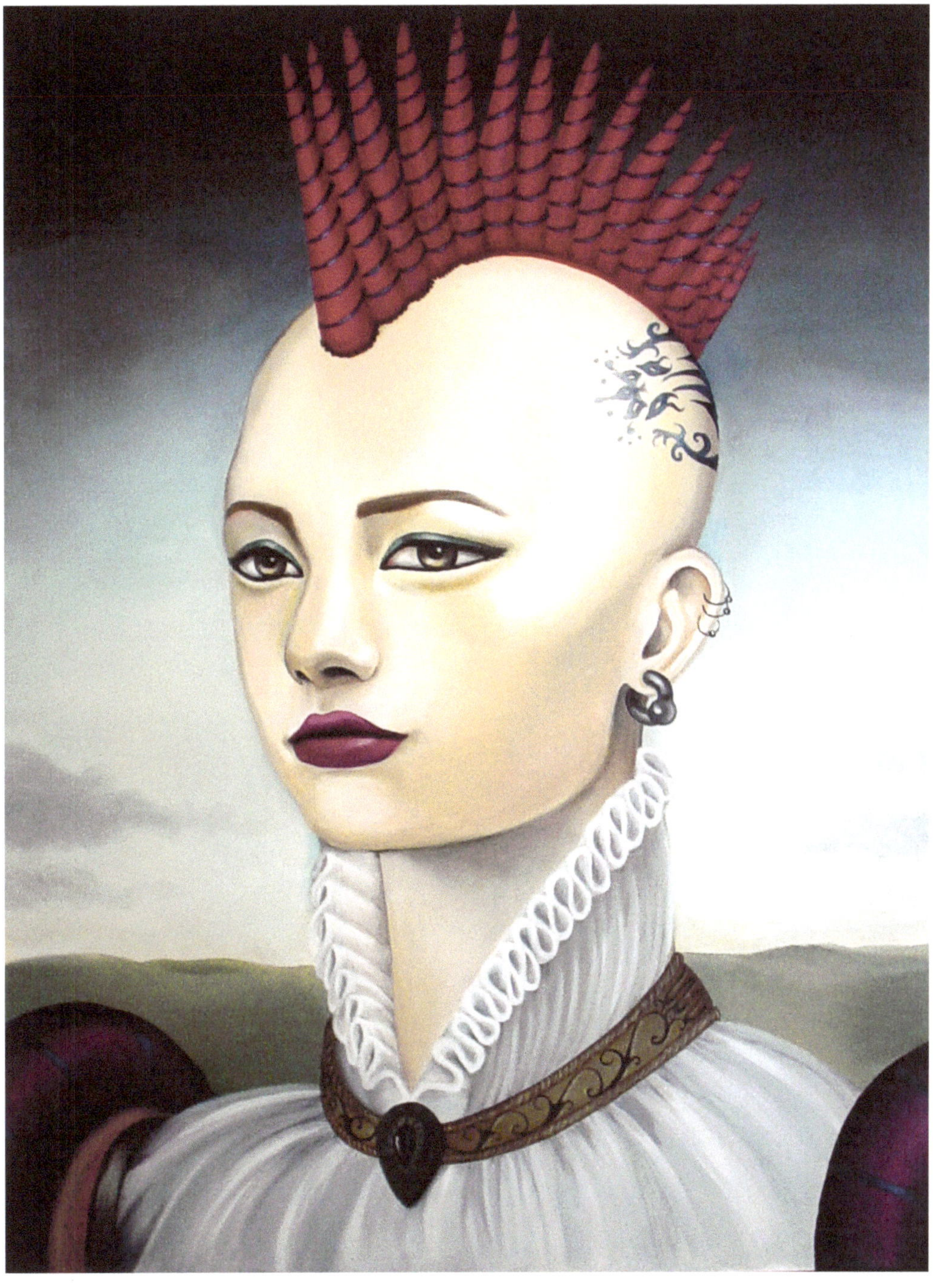

11 x 14" OIL ON PANEL

Laszlo, Duke of Scovelica (1510–1580)

The largest private landowner in Kessa and a cousin to the King. Though he was the subject of much envy, he was known to be shy and socialized rarely, preferring to put important decisions in the hands of the chancellor. His child bride would inspire him to pursue writing prose and philosophy as occupations.

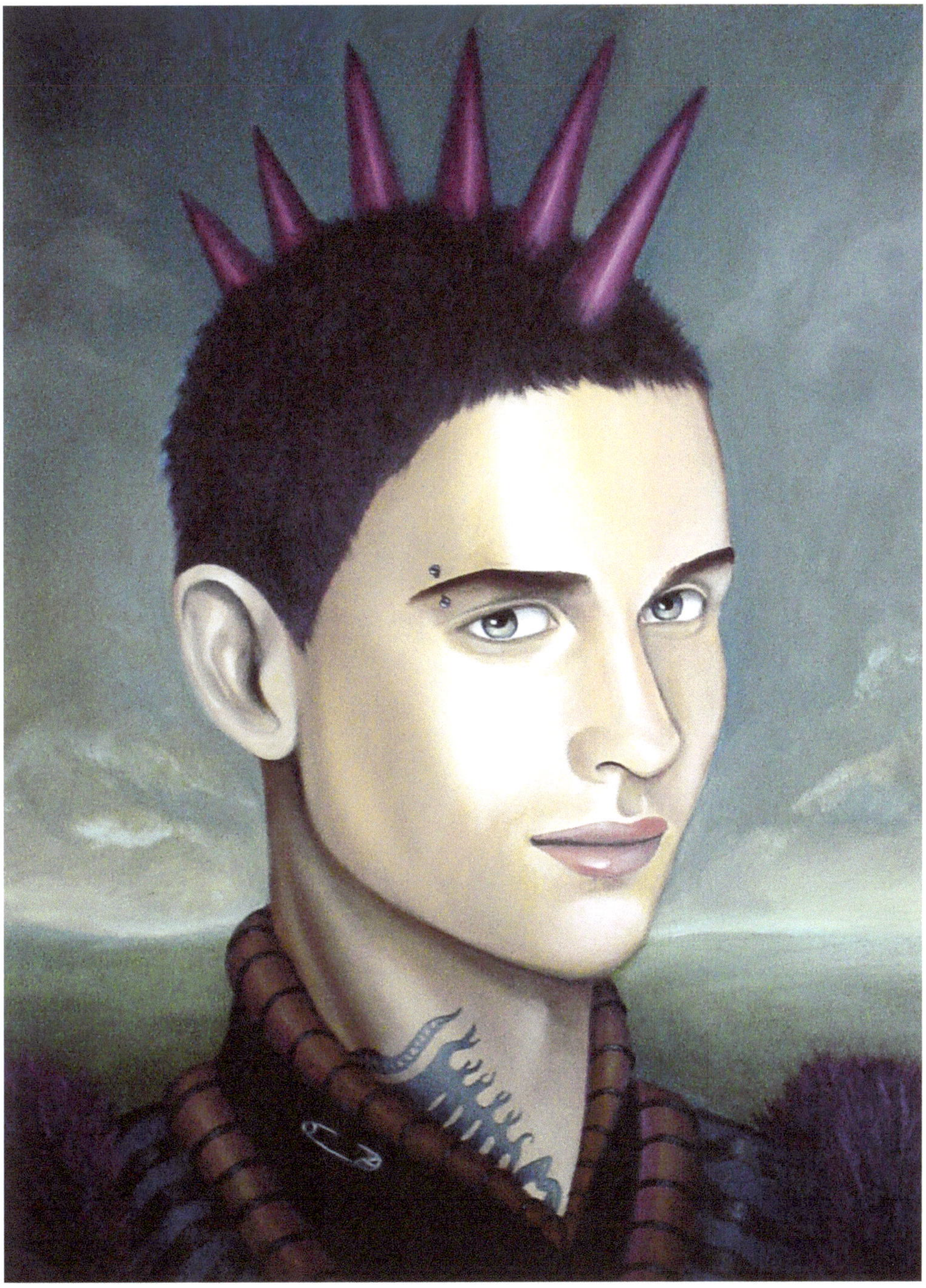

11 x 14" OIL ON PANEL

Lady Evangeline (1523–1564)

Second daughter to the Duke and Duchess of Scovelica, she very rarely did much of anything beyond hunting or pursuing the other outdoor activities she so loved. Despite her beauty and family attempts at turning her into a 'dignified lady', she tried with great effort to mask her femininity. She swore like a sailor, preferred the hardest of liquor and loved to roll around in dirt with her five wolfhounds. Though pursued by eligible men in the horse and hound set, she would never marry.

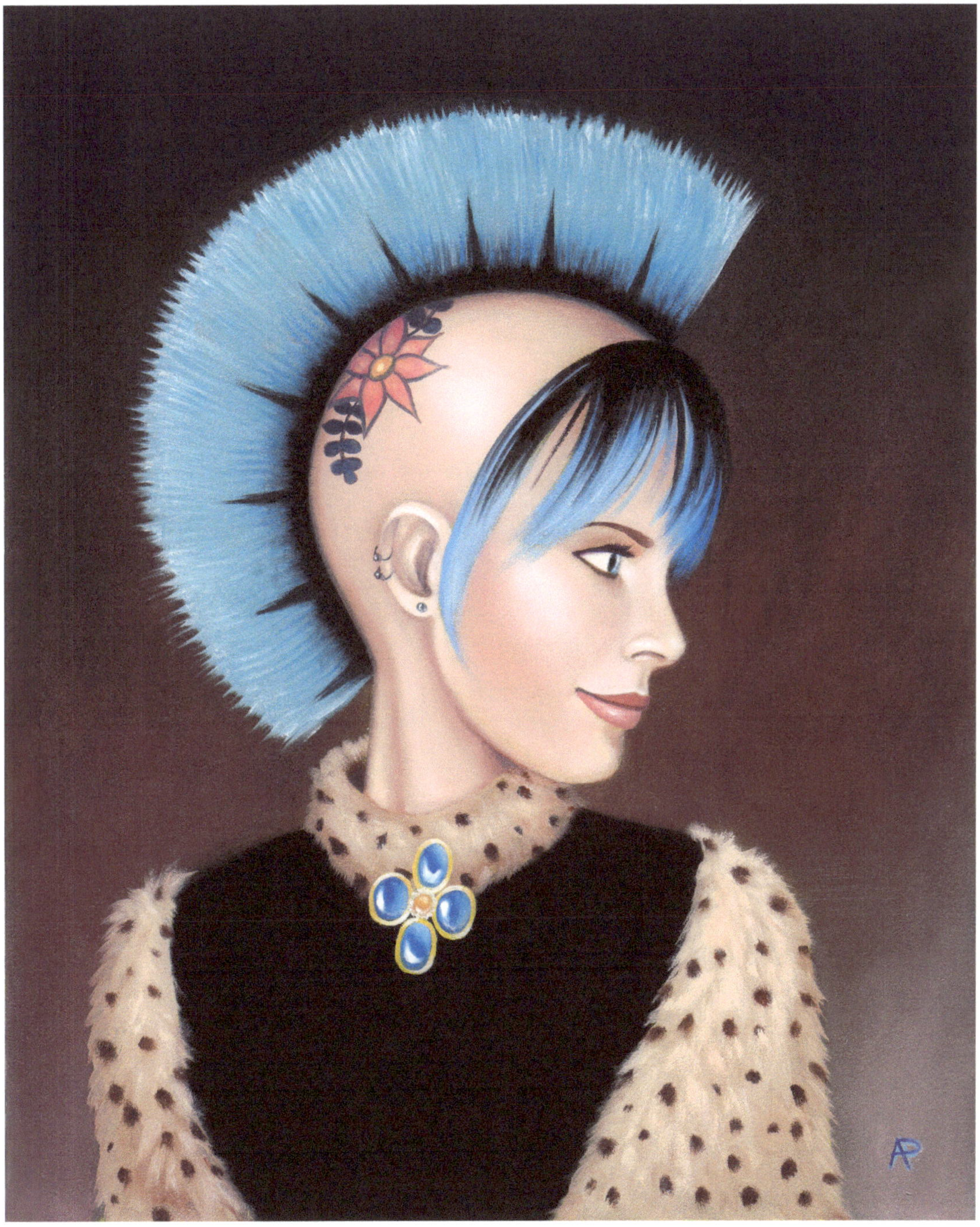

8 x 10" oil on panel

Beatrice, Duchess of Bruenza (1527–1589)

First daughter of the Duke and Duchess of Scovelica, she was known as much for her lavish finery as the powerful ancestors she came from. Where her parents had been reluctant about their duties, Beatrice was haughty, imperious, and had political aspirations. Marrying the Duke of Bruenza in 1550, motherhood softened political hopes into that of becoming a playwright. When her first play resulted in oceans of angry spitting from the audience, she settled for being a curtain puller.

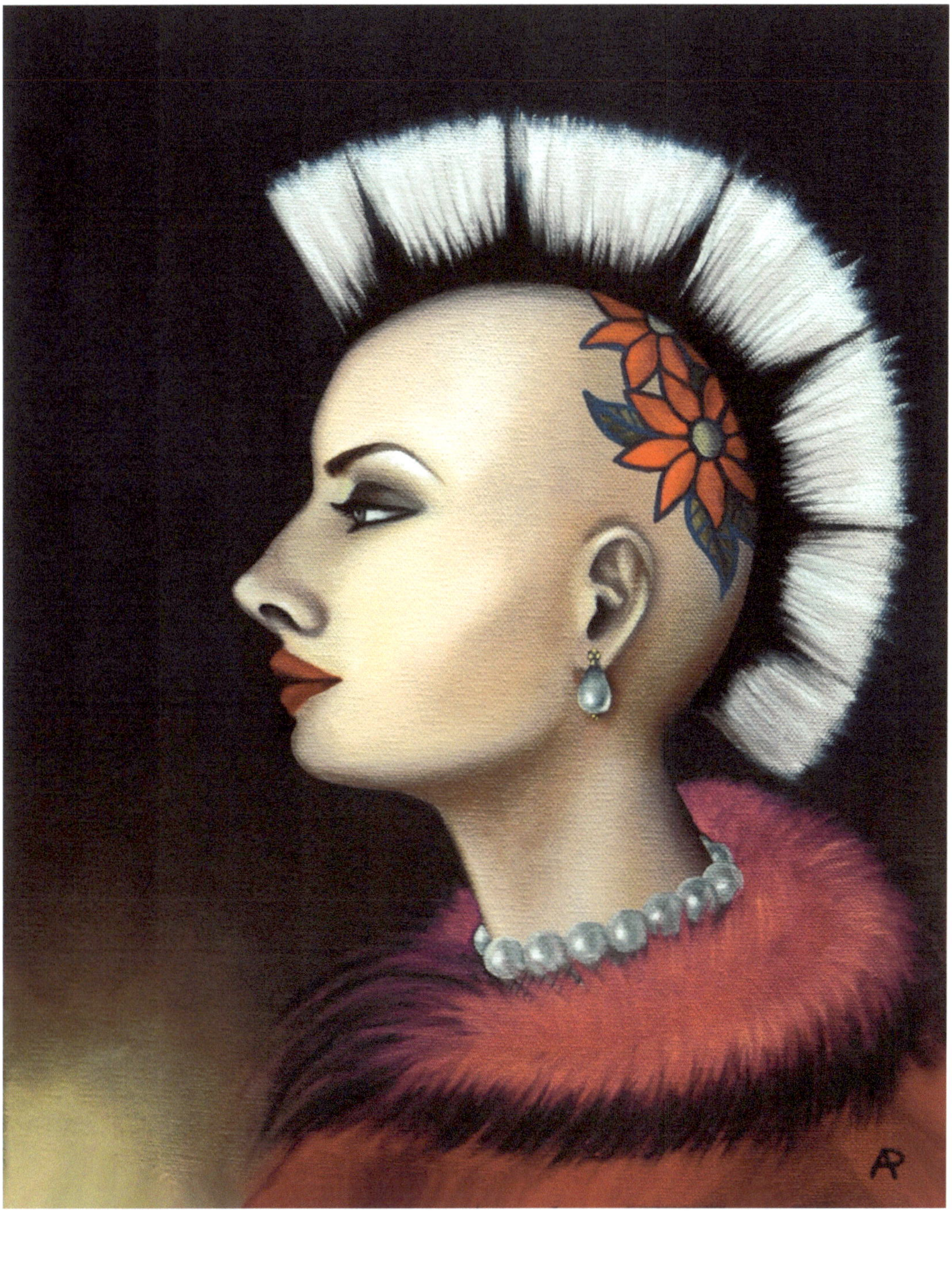

11 x 14" OIL ON CANVAS

Lady Alexis of Veron (1556–unknown)

Married at age 15 to Lord Armand, second son of the Duke and Duchess of Bruenza. She was the daughter of an architect with a gambling problem, a problem great enough that she was handed over to Armand to settle a debt. Though she was spoiled and doted on, treated more as a daughter than a wife, the years of her fundamental discontent ended with a decision to run away with a harpsichord player she had hired as dinner party entertainment.

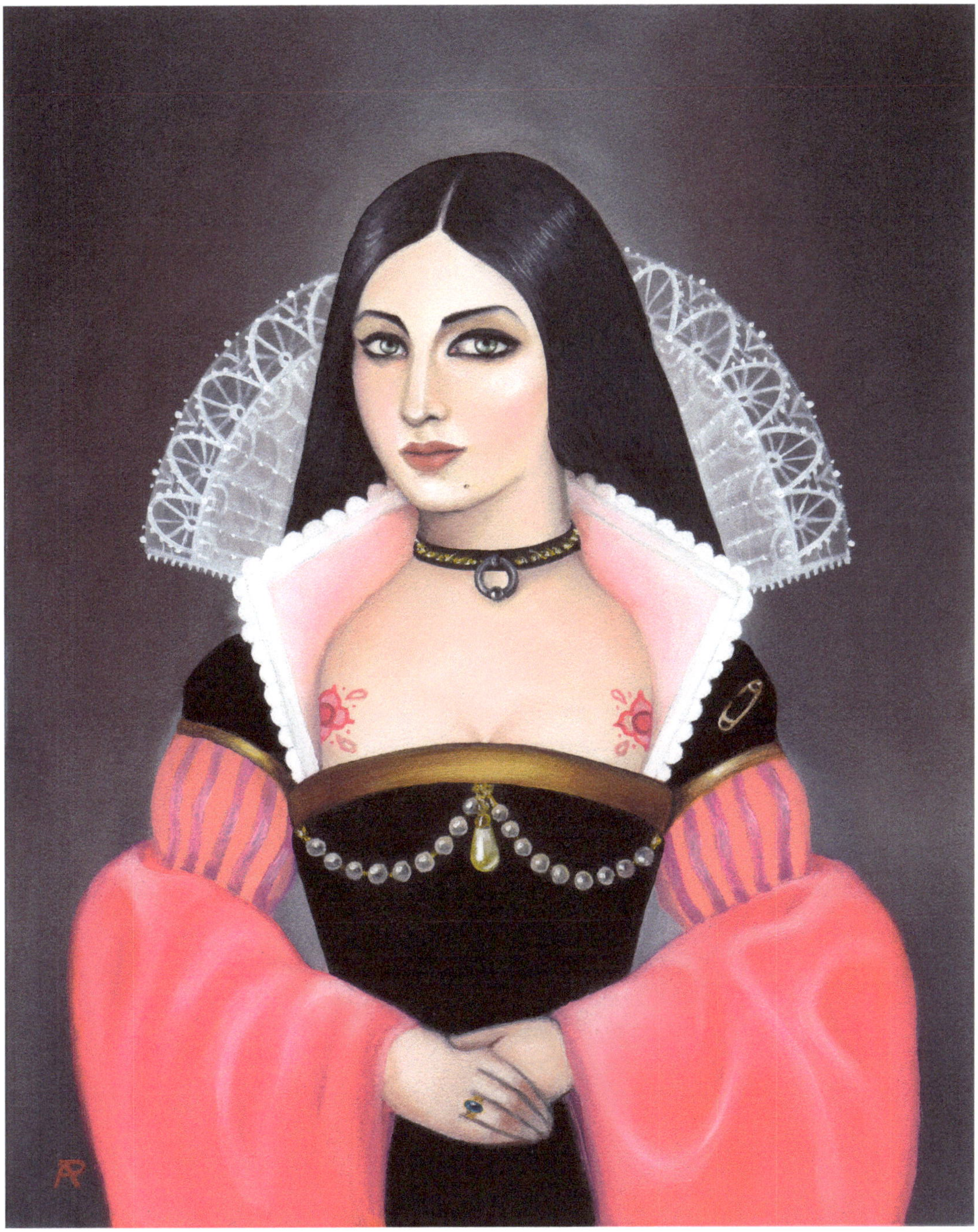

8 x 10" oil on panel

Lord Leo of Brammen (1442–1502)

Marrying Lucrezia de Terra in 1473, he was famous for the building of his elaborate country estate, Barrole Hall. A mammoth testament to his ego, credibility, power, and – perhaps an attempt at immortality – several were killed during its construction. It was after the great house was completed that his wife and sons went missing off the coast of Egypt. He commissioned a marble statue of a giraffe to be placed at the front gates of Barrole in their honor.

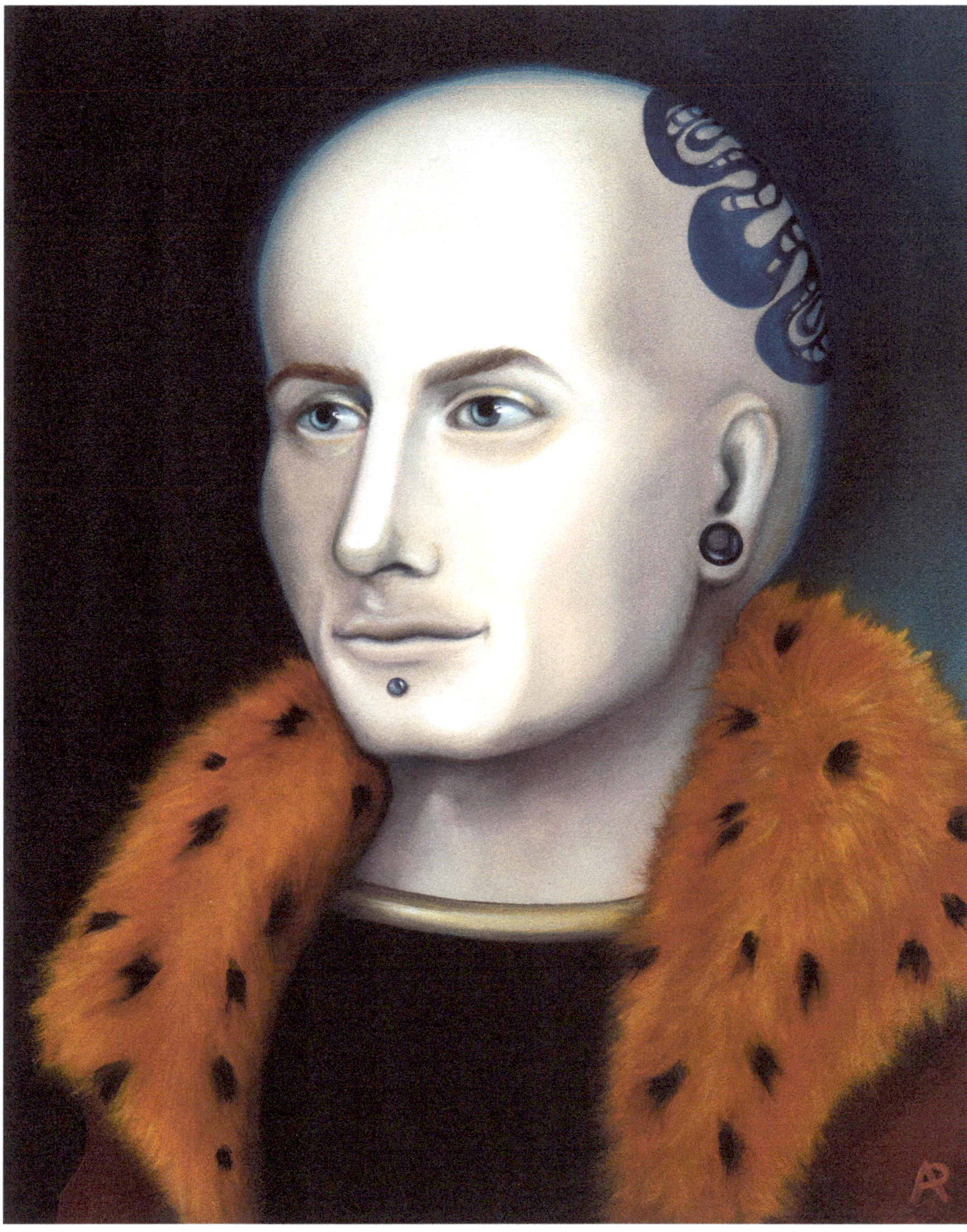

8 x 10" OIL ON PANEL

LADY LUCREZIA DE TERRA (1451–1489)

A dry sense of duty with a taste for theatrics and travel, her father was Master of Protocol to the King. To be included in her circle was coveted. On a trip with her three eldest sons to buy several pet giraffes for their country estate, their ship was later found destroyed on the shores of Egypt.

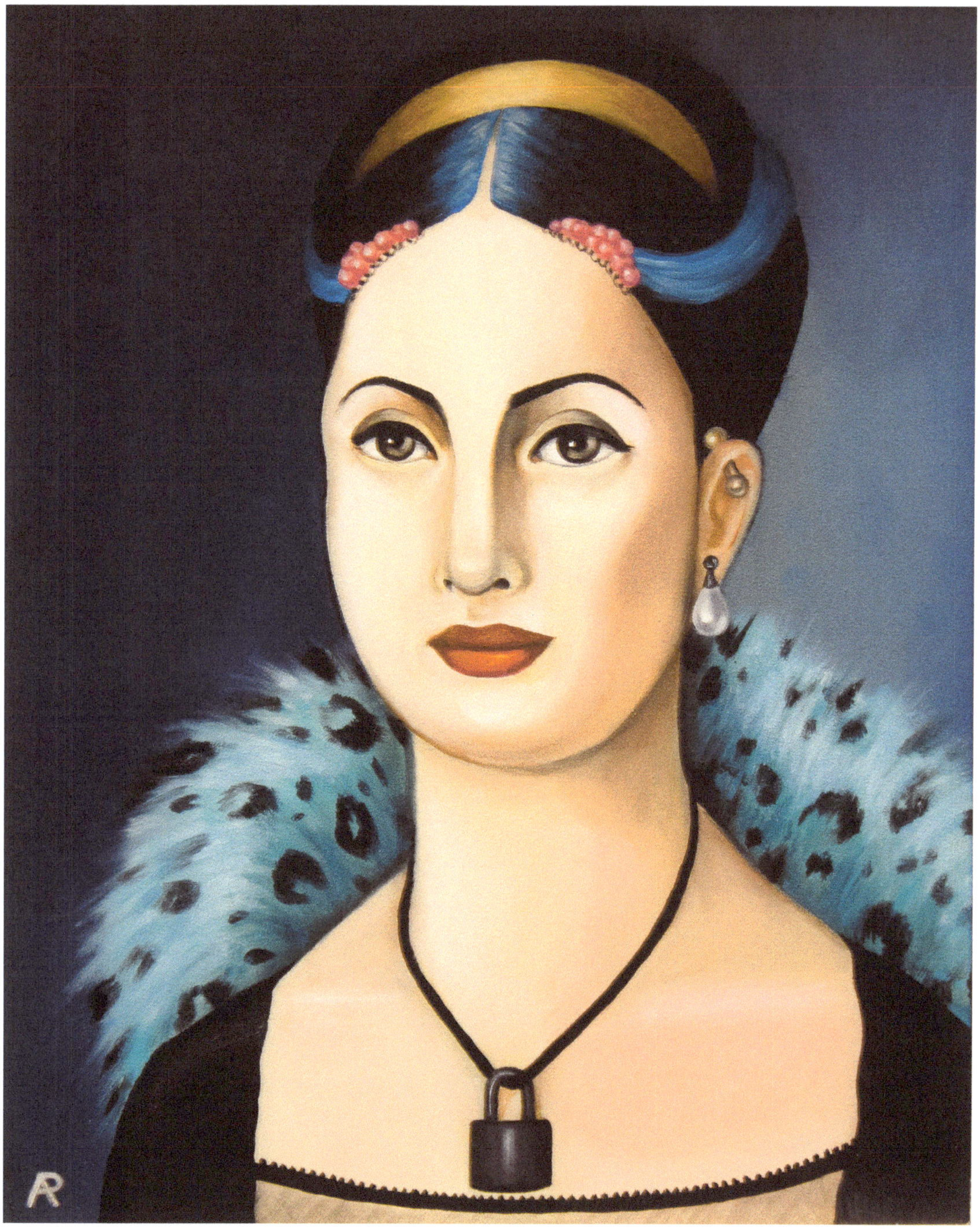

8 x 10" OIL ON PANEL

Simon the Earl of Luc (1504–1572)

Described as honorable and of a winning disposition, the Earl would become master of Barrole Hall and a collector of weaponry from various cultures. After a few animated and enthusiastic demonstrations with other collectors and military men resulted in "accidents", liquor was banned at his home. His collection stayed intact at Barrole Hall until 1802, when it was looted during the Civil War.

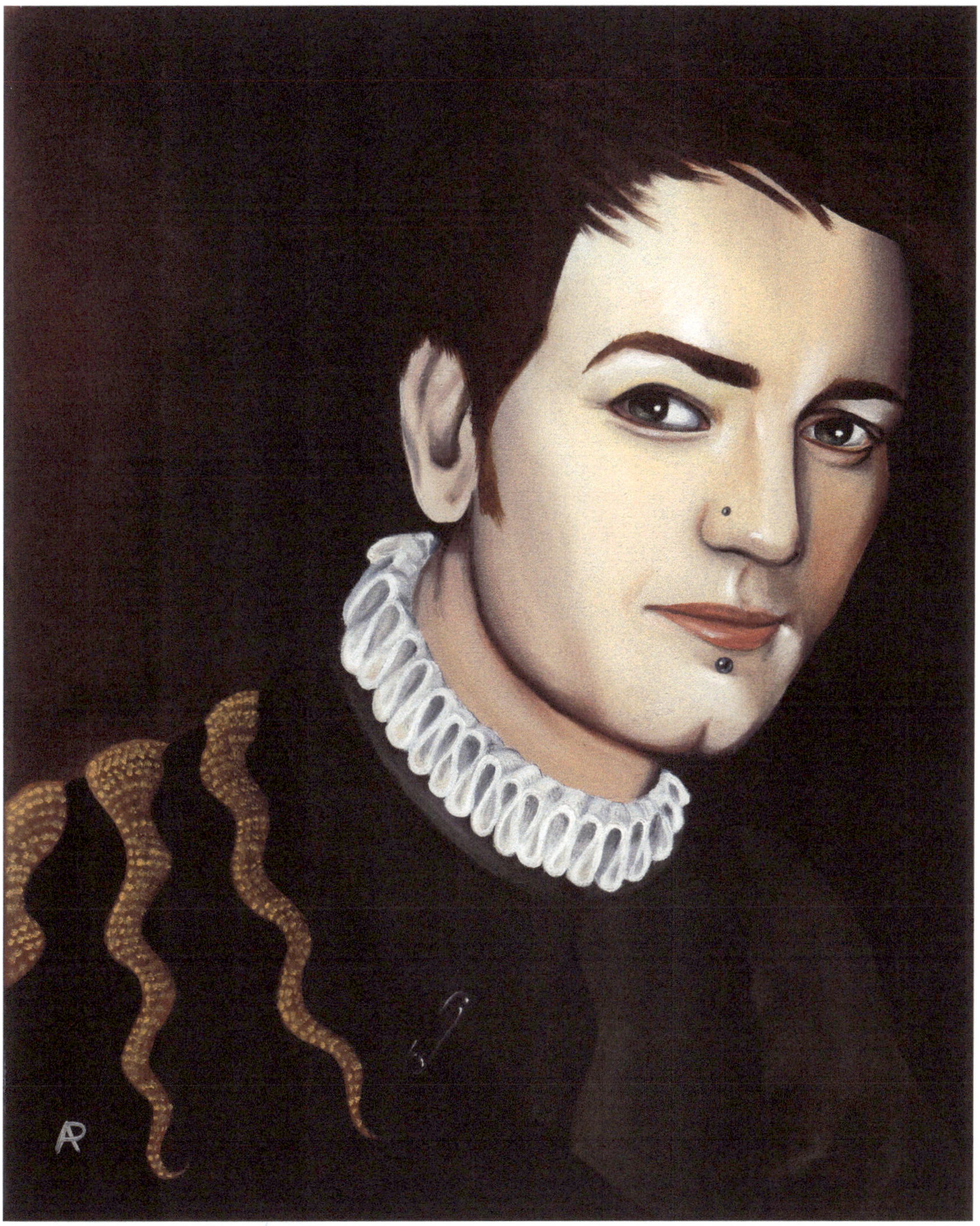

8 x 10" OIL ON PANEL

Alexia de Luc (1503–1577)

Starting her career at 17 as the mistress to a string of prominent political figures, she married the Earl of Luc in 1523. Acquiring a title and a large estate, she emanated an aura of majesty. She thus became a patron of sorts, funneling money into publications that would support the agenda of former lovers.

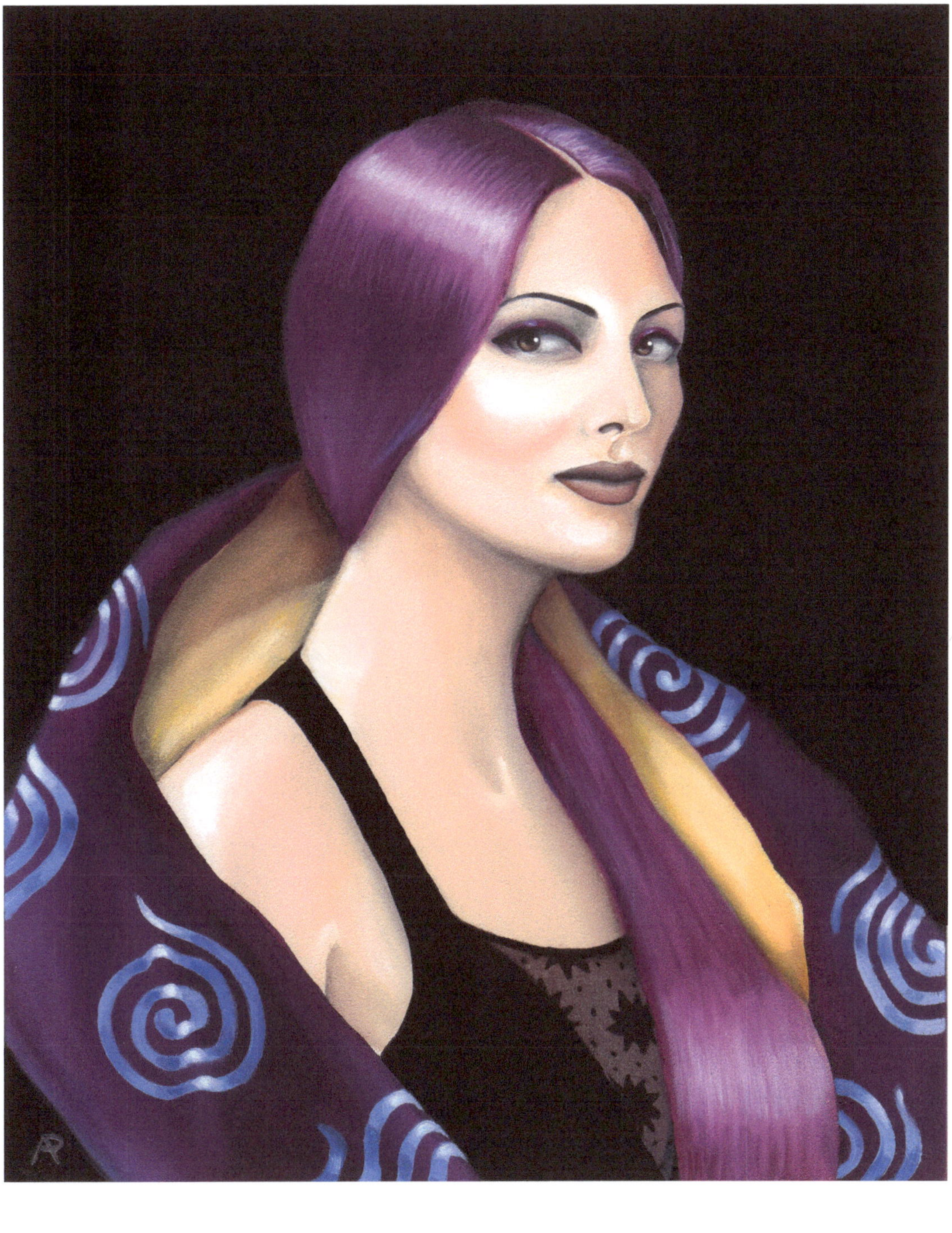

8 x 10" oil on panel

Nayanna of Alia, Countess of Luc (1527–1586)

The chance to marry "well" came thanks to the lucrative family lumber business, and two uncles who served as tutors to a succession of royal children. Marrying the second Earl of Luc and becoming mistress of Barrole Hall, she had a son – fulfilling her expectation. The countess conducted her life autonomously; the earl was hardly to be found, a ghost moving in the background of her life while he hunted, traveled, and philandered. Keeping the chattels of Barrole Hall in tact, her additions to the home became a triumph of original bad taste. The madness of her egomania revealed itself in mixes of Oriental, Greek, Venetian renaissance, bronze statues draped with silver lame, and her collection of wax dolls. Nayanna would gain notoriety later, as a widow, when her majordomo of 30 years appeared next her to bedside stark naked and professed his love, she replied, "don't be stupid, and put that awful thing away!" He promptly retrieved a cross-bow and shot himself between the eyes. Nayanna was most distressed about replacing her rare, and now blood stained, Oriental rug.

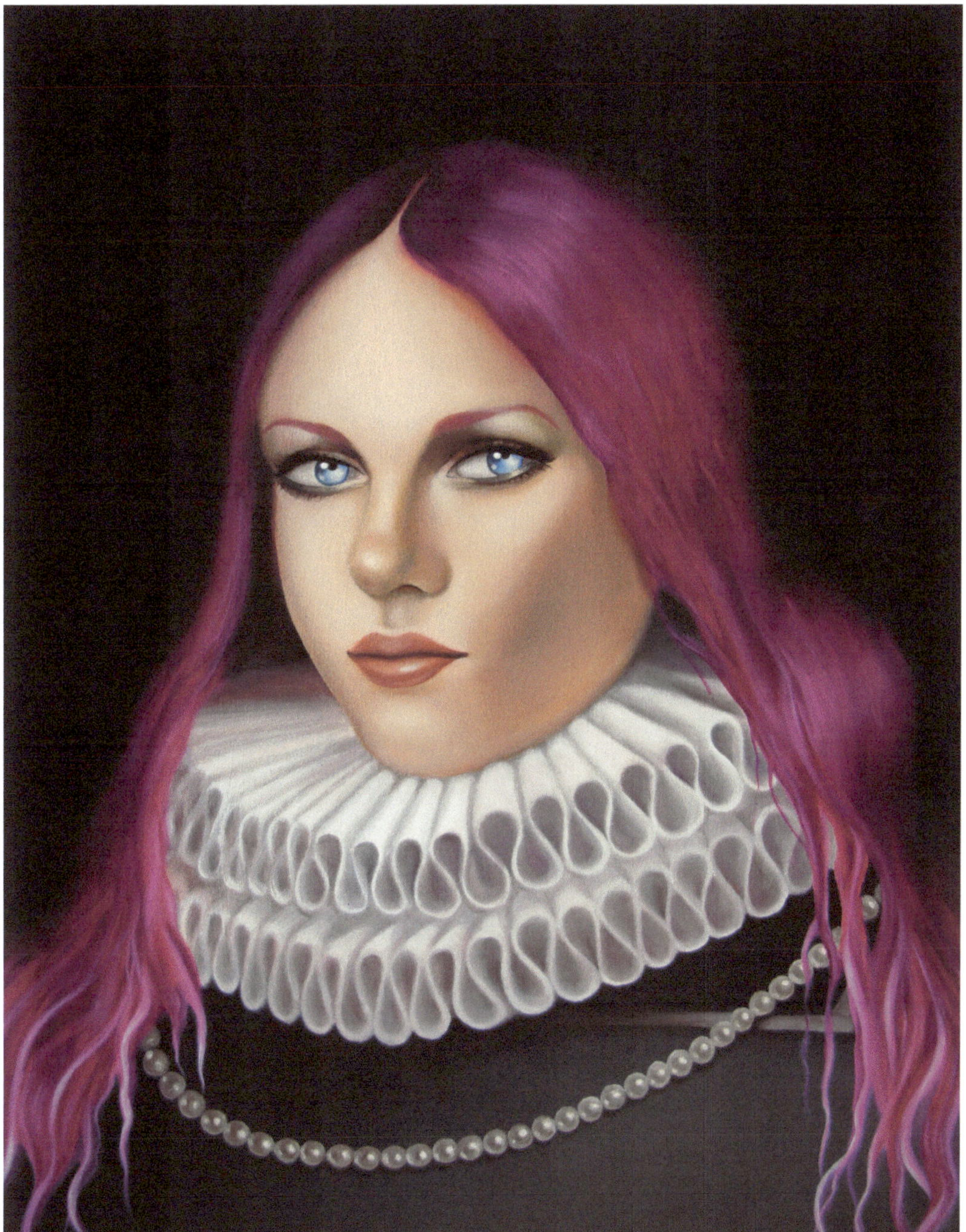

11 x 14" OIL ON PANEL

Dinara of Terra (1558–1600)

Known for having the ability to possess both a serene dignity, and crassness matched only by drunken rogues, she was able to balance her duties as a Lady while indulging her rebellious nature. It was said the aura of graciousness could lessen even the most audacious remark or action. Perhaps this is why the 3rd Earl of Luc found himself proposing marriage, even after thwarted attempts and sarcastic insults. Upon meeting the earl Dinara stated curtly during a dinner party, "I hear that all earls have tiny penises, do you find this to be true?" Whether true or not, three children would come as a result of their nuptials.

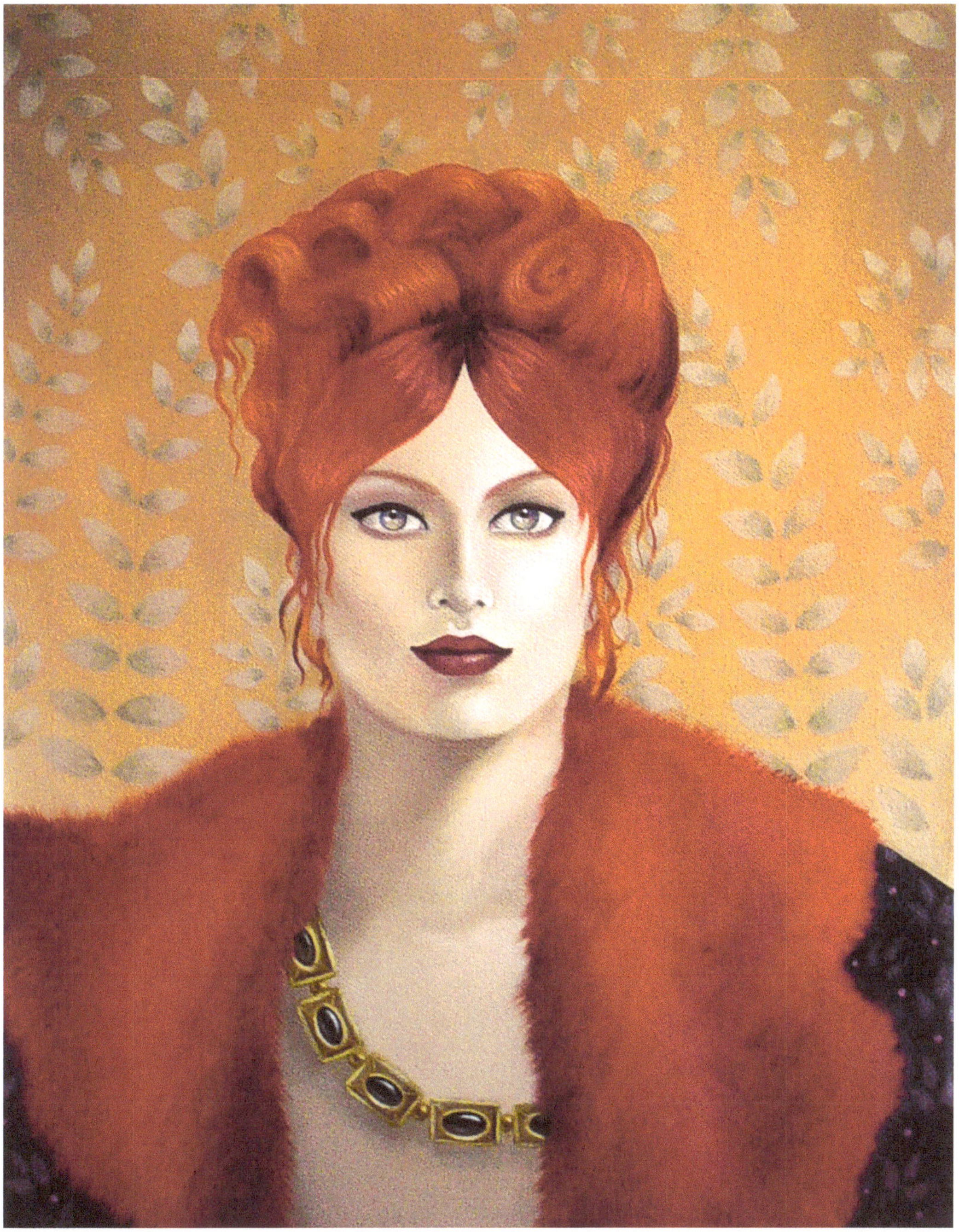

11 x 14" OIL ON CANVAS

Violanté, Duchess of Mollawray (1578–1650)

After the sudden death of her husband Henri the 2nd Duke of Mollowray in a hunting accident, she went into a lifetime of mourning. She stopped dying her hair and powdered her face a ghostly white to show that she herself was now living-dead. Little did she know this would spark a fashion trend; women stopped dying their hair for nearly forty years.

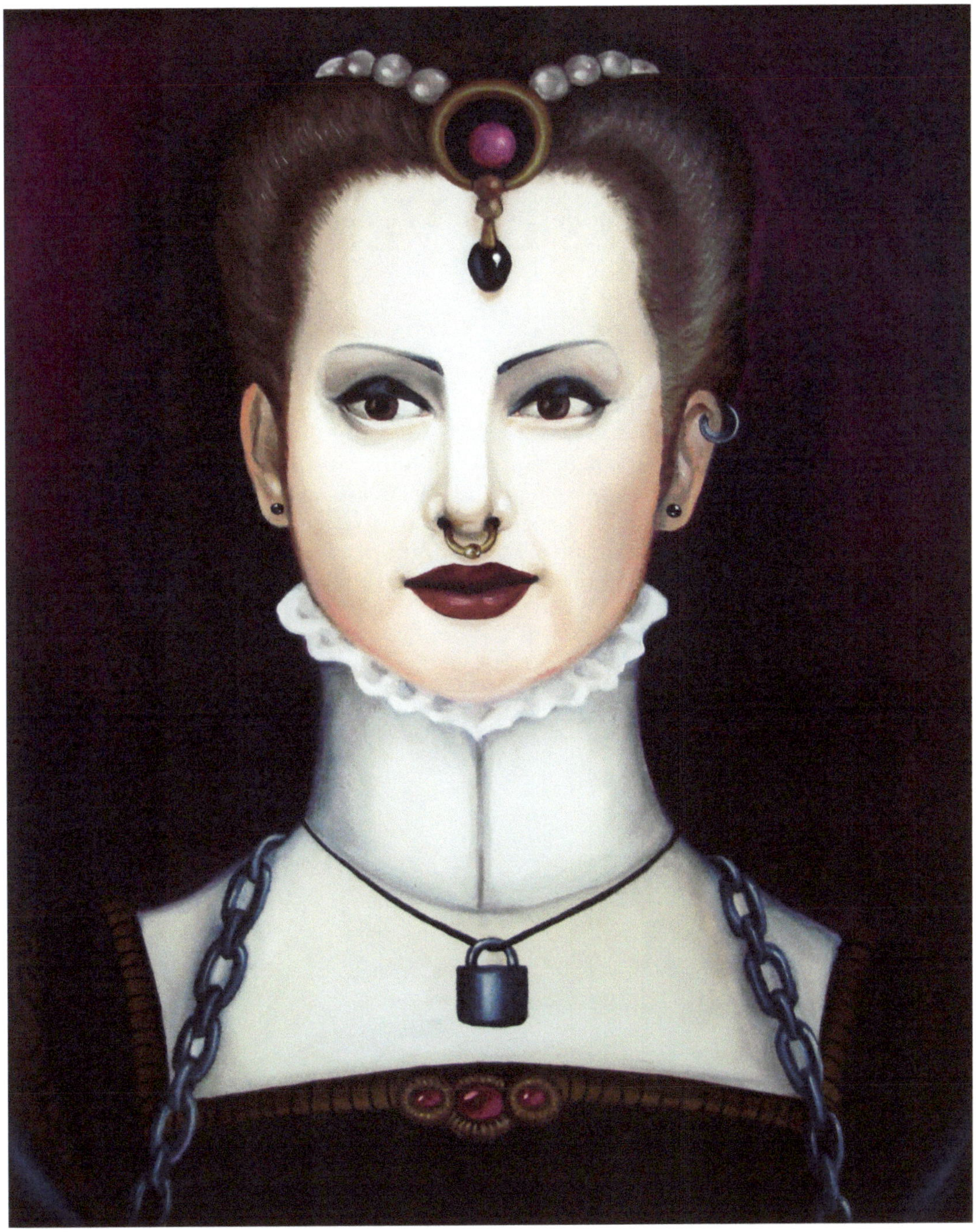

8 x 10" OIL ON PANEL

Christabelle, Countess of Veron (1612–1667)

Second daughter to the 3rd Duke of Mollawray. Like her sister, Lexia, she had a penchant for spending and married late to the Earl of Veron in 1645. Developing an interest in astrology, séances and the occult, she had her estate redecorated with astrological motifs and even converted her main parlor into a "room for the dead" in which to summon ghosts. She said she found the dead more interesting than the living.

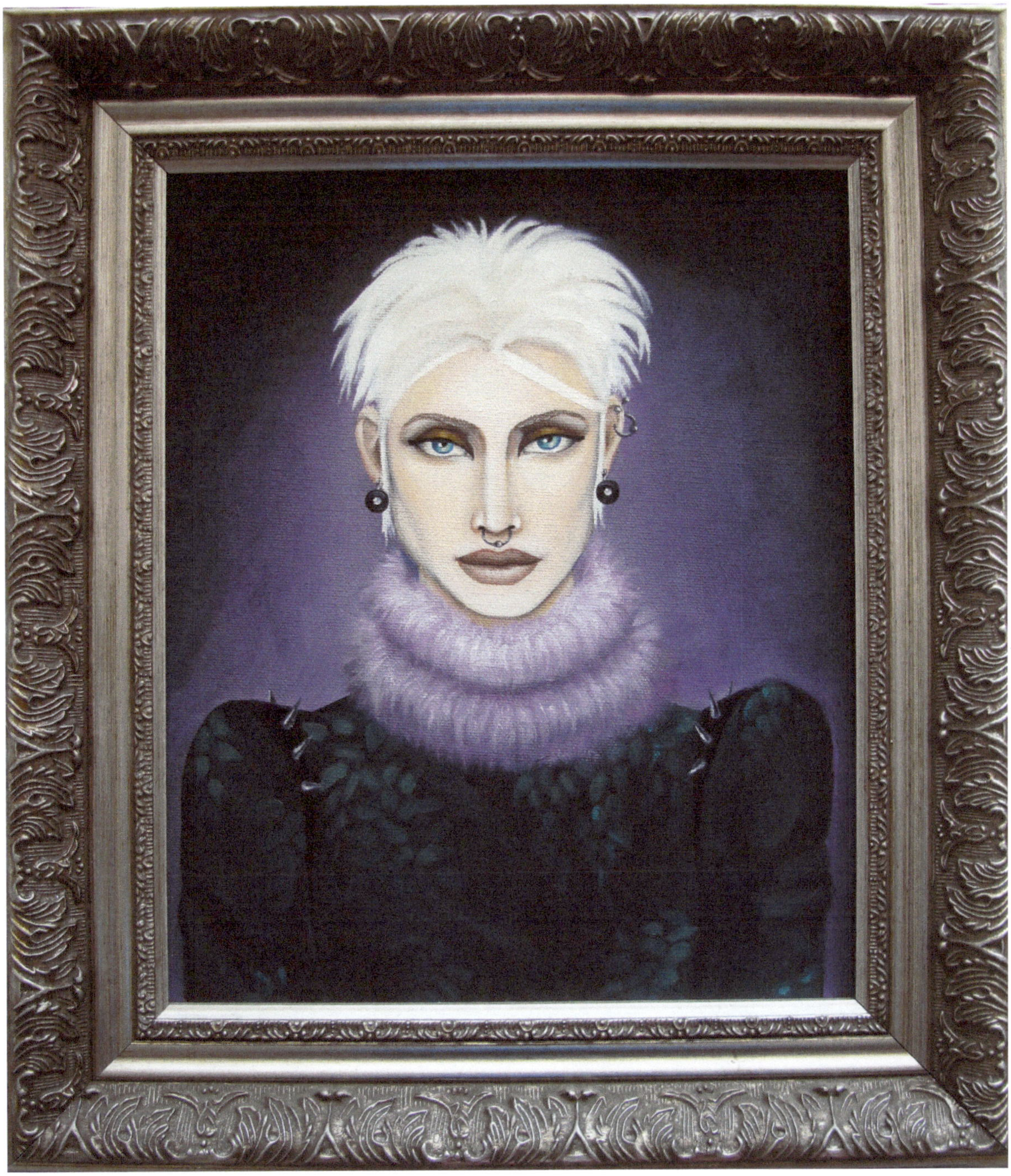

11 x 14" oil on canvas

Augustus, Earl of Veron (1592–1662)

Brought up in the highest court after the death of his parents, he rose in ranks of the army and was sent on many important diplomatic missions. Despite judging allies with their ability to agree with him and being an insufferable know-it-all, he became a chief minister. Accomplishing much at an early age, he married Christabelle, a woman twenty years his senior. He took strange pleasure in her always calling him "young man" in both public and private moments.

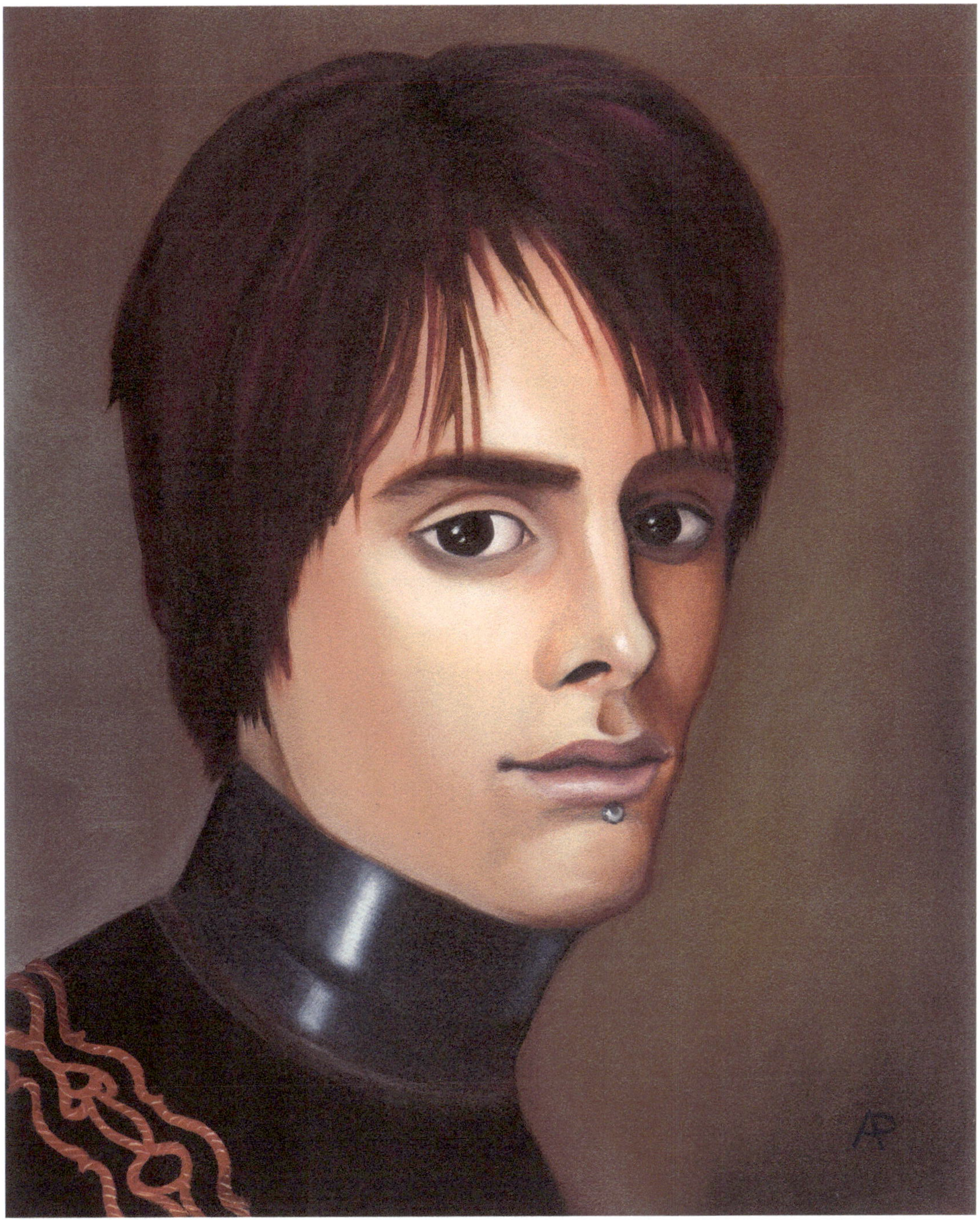

8 x 10" oil on panel

Lady Justine
(1568–1639)

The illegitimate daughter of the Duke of Mollawray, her early years are a mystery before a brief reconciliation with her father before his death, and subsequent arranged marriage to an abusive Lord Lieutenant, 40 years older than her. After her husband died – rumored to have been poisoned – and remarkably able to keep his estate, she presided over her tenants and lands to the best of her ability and was found to be charming and gracious. The only thing ever that could be said that was odd, was her penchant for lining up her staff every morning and spanking each one with her hair brush; she reasoned this was punishment for the sins they might commit that day. While this caused a great turnover in maids and housekeepers, much of her male staff remained faithful, and seemed to look forward to this bit of protocol.

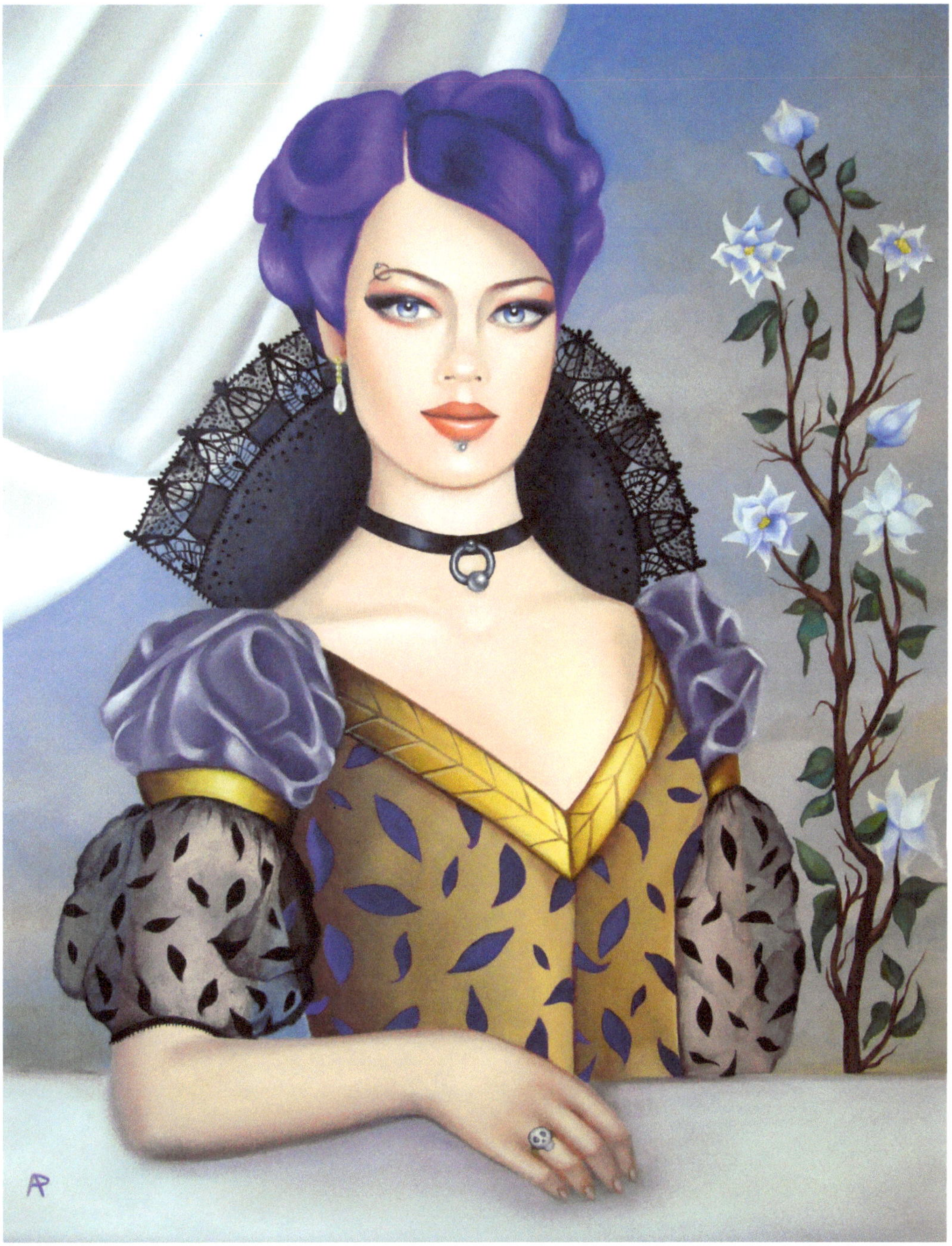

11 X 14" OIL ON PANEL

Lexia, Marquise of Vienwray (1608–1674)

First daughter to the 3rd Duke of Mollowray. A reputation for beauty and gambling, she was content to marry late at age 34 to the Marquess of Vienwray - much to her father's relief. Her clothing and extensive jewelry collection was legendary, for her husband saw her as a showpiece as much as a wife. Copies of her jewelry were made well into the 19th Century and are a source of inspiration for designers even today.

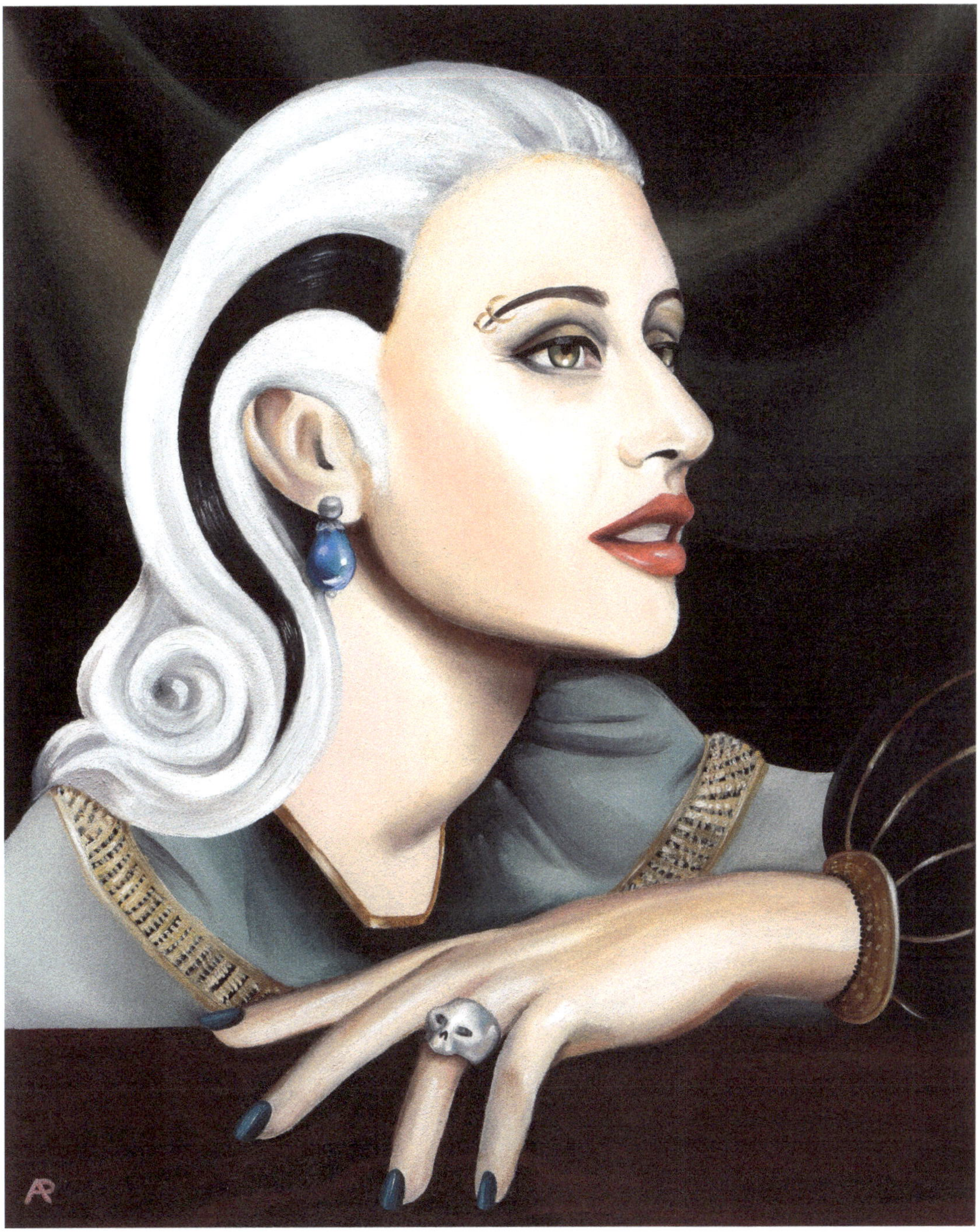

8 x 10" OIL ON PANEL

Adolfus, Marquess of Vienwray (1610–1687)

Known as difficult, reclusive yet charming when the time suited him, his penchant for gambling led to his marrying Lexia, not only for her beauty and reputation, but her social prowess as a means to mask his own short-comings both social and political. In time, however, he became disenchanted with humanity and retreated from public life.

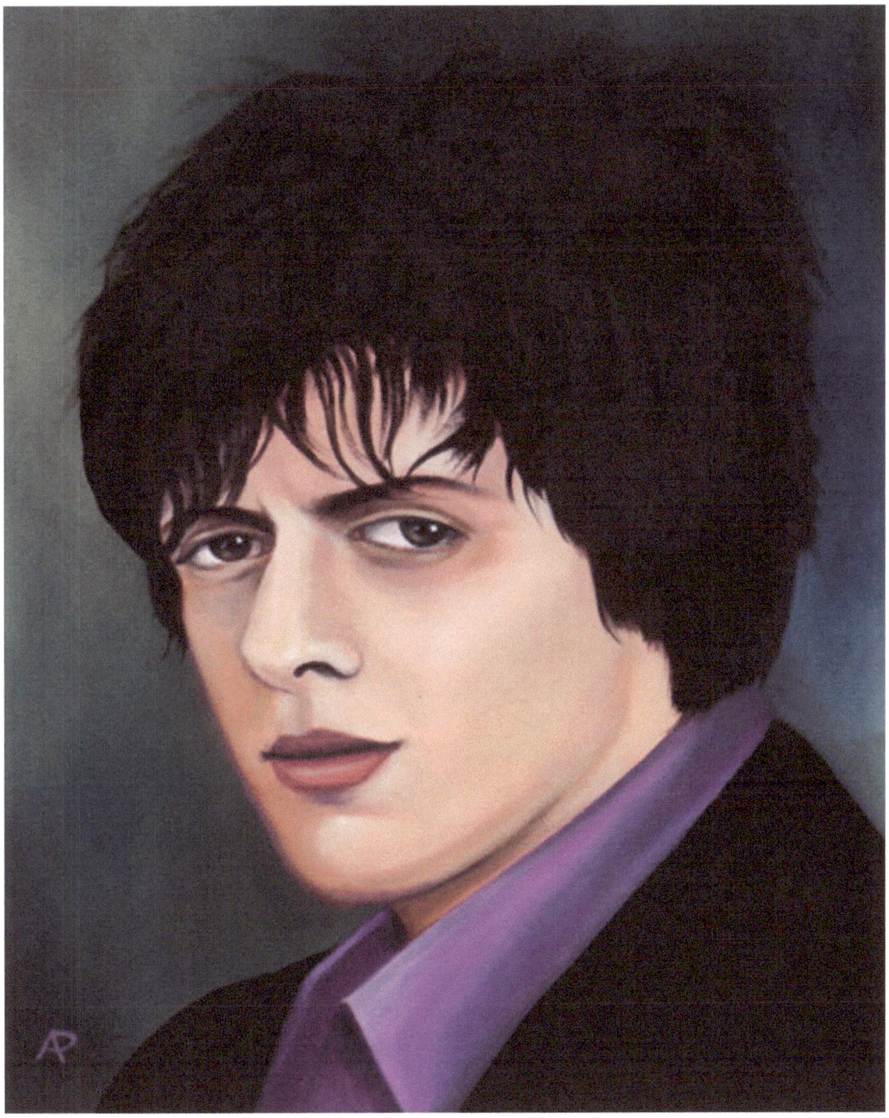

8 x 10" OIL ON PANEL

Jaecine, Countess of Albramere (1709–1777)

The Countess came from a prominent family that owned several wool and textile mills. A friend of artists, she began designing her own draperies, linens, and fabrics to suite her aesthetic and other prominent women with large houses. Using her husband's funds and the family factories she later created The House of Albramere, a largely successful venture as manufacturer and seller of fine linens to the fashionable and wealthy.

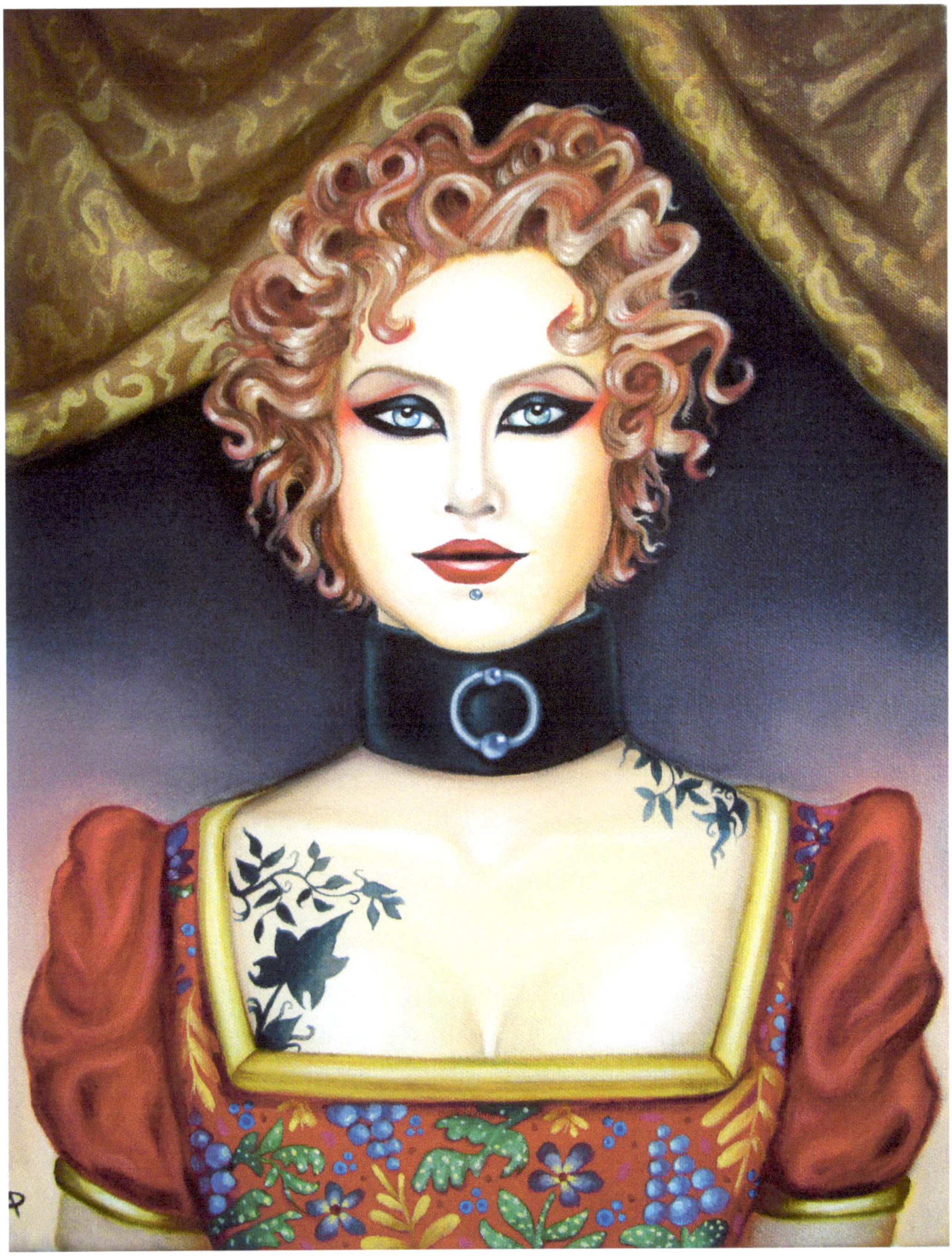

11 x 14" OIL ON CANVAS

Latis, Earl of Vienwray (1728–1758)

Described as an affable and talented man, his passion for the outdoors and philanthropy made him very popular among the well, and not so well, to-do population of Vienwray. Women were another passion, one that turned deadly. At age 30 he was found in bed with a slit throat, the handy work of a jealous servant with whom he been having an affair.

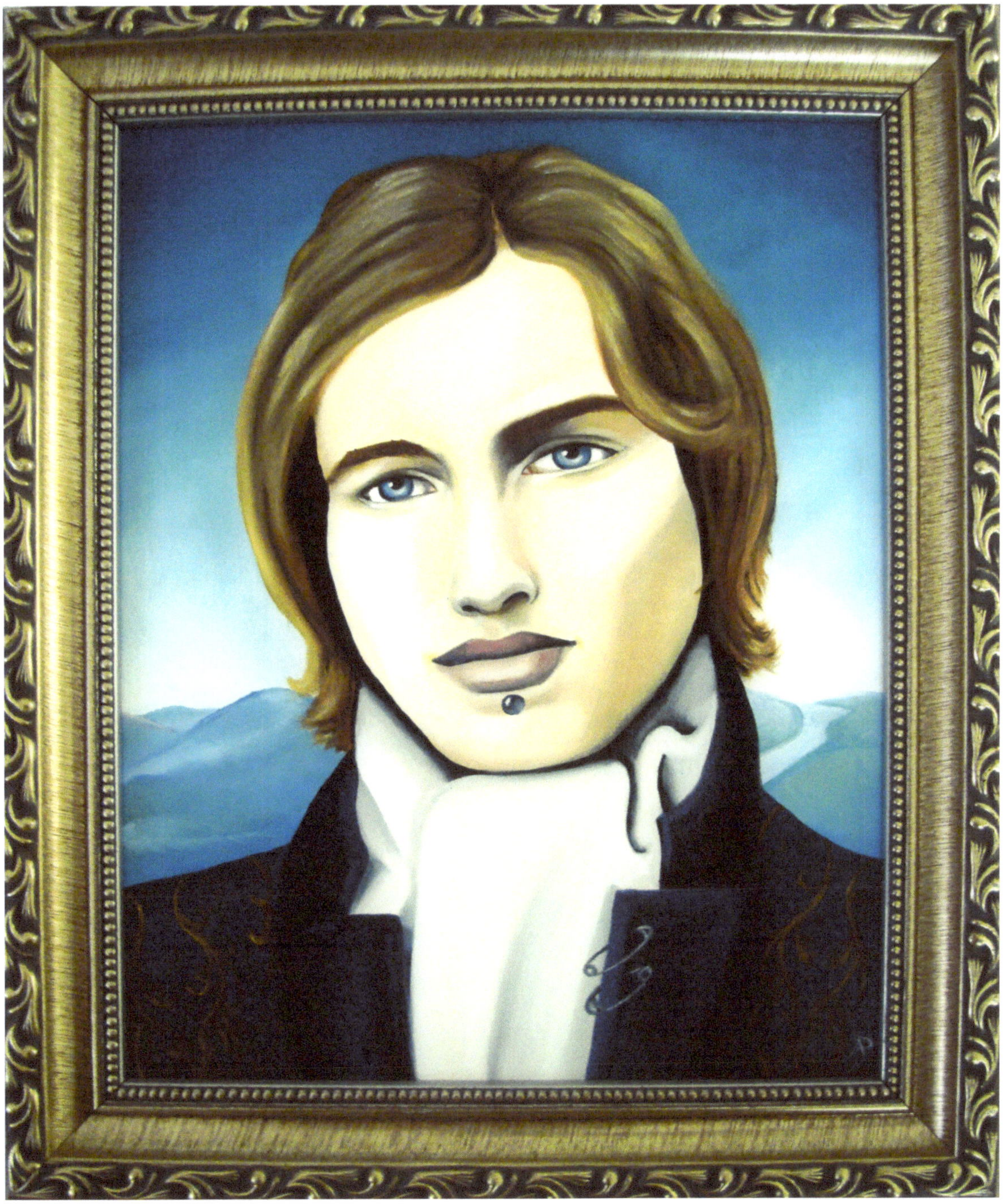

8 x 10" OIL ON PANEL

Lady Christina of Albramere, Countess of Vienwray (1730–1778)

The daughter of an eminent Lord, she was described as a high priestess of social arts. A formidable woman with a desire for perfection in every facet of her life, she ran her establishment with precision and luxury. Her clothes, her home, her friends and her children were all perfect, as she could expect no less. Despite having achieved perfection, her husband strayed not only to women such as servants in their own home, but to Christina's own sister, Lady Marcella.

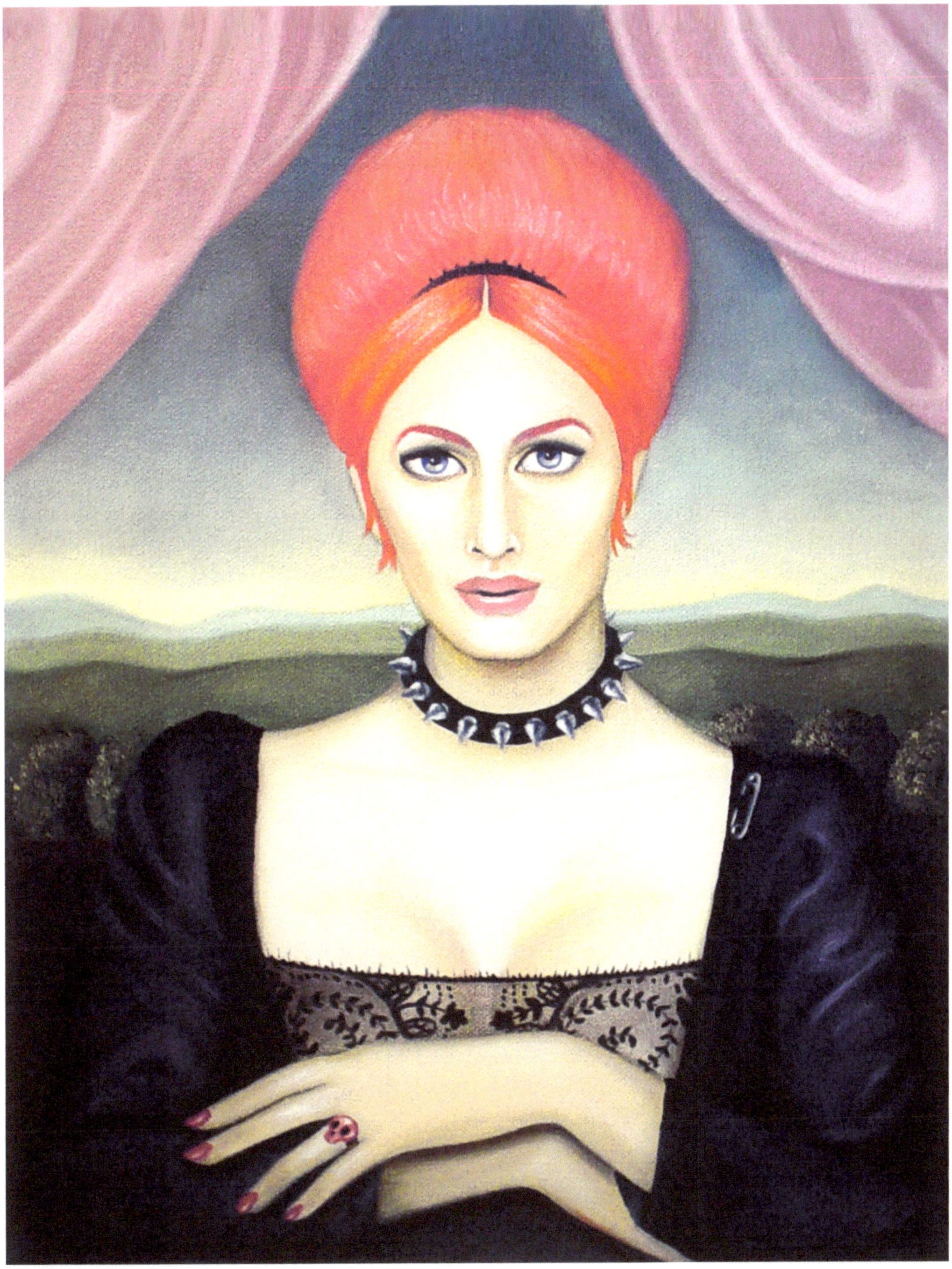

11 x 14" OIL ON CANVAS

Lady Marcella of Albramere (1734–1790)

Along with her sisters, including the Countess of Vienwray, the "girls from Albramere" were well known among the fashionable set and a great source of gossip. Raised in every way to be a coveted show piece for a deserving royal member, Marcella was accomplished in everything from sailing to sewing. She was also a keen collector of men, which included the husbands of her sisters. She reasoned that men were like wardrobes, "every season I get a new set".

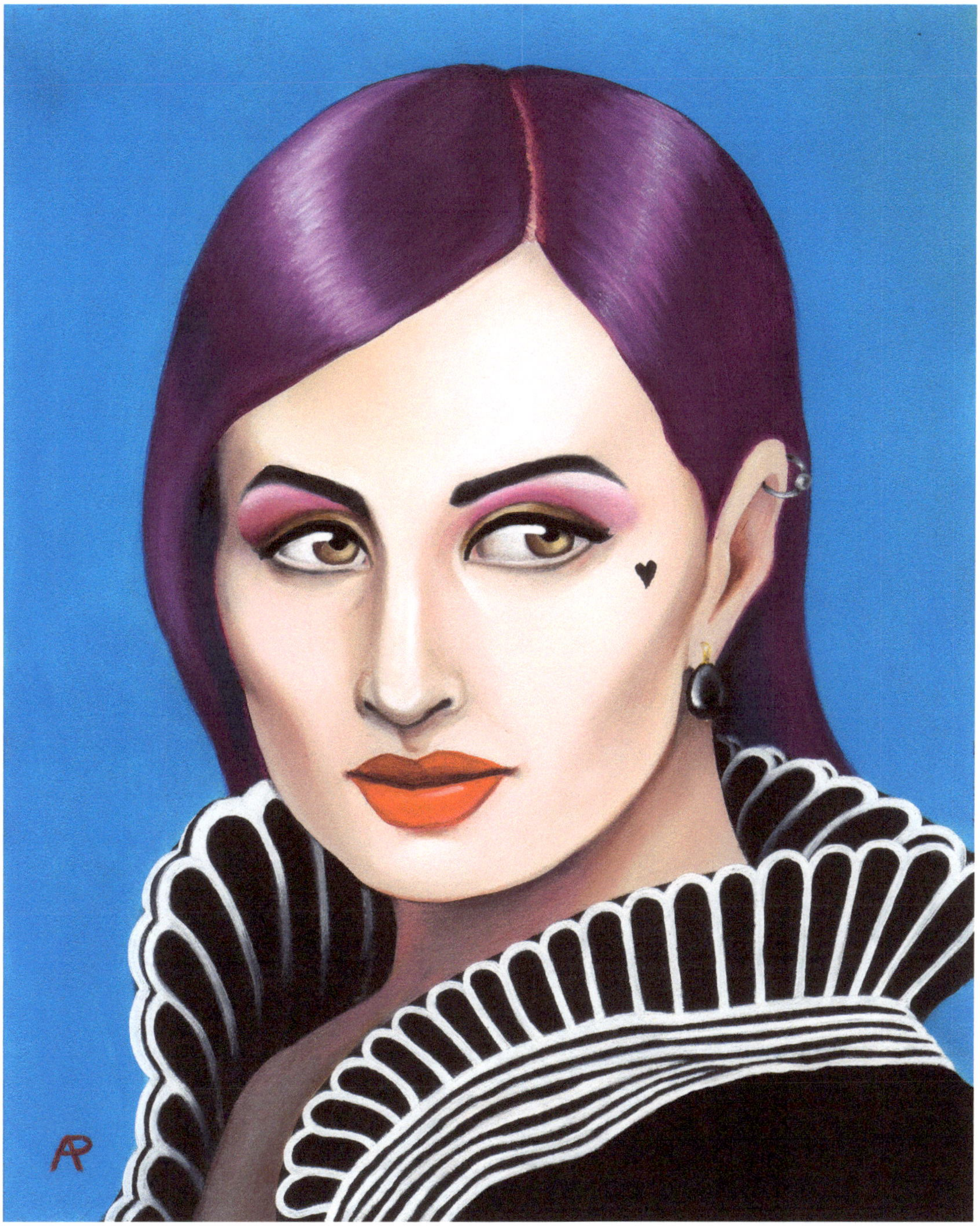

8 x 10" oil on panel

Ingrid
(1774–1840)

A unique and sweet tempered viola prodigy, her effortless talent would send her playing with the best instructors, composers and operas. Despite this, she lacked direction and was a slave to boredom, thus turning her mentors and admirers in the music world into brief lovers. Losing her stamina, she was blessed with an inherited fortune and spent her later years composing unfinished songs and languishing in bed.

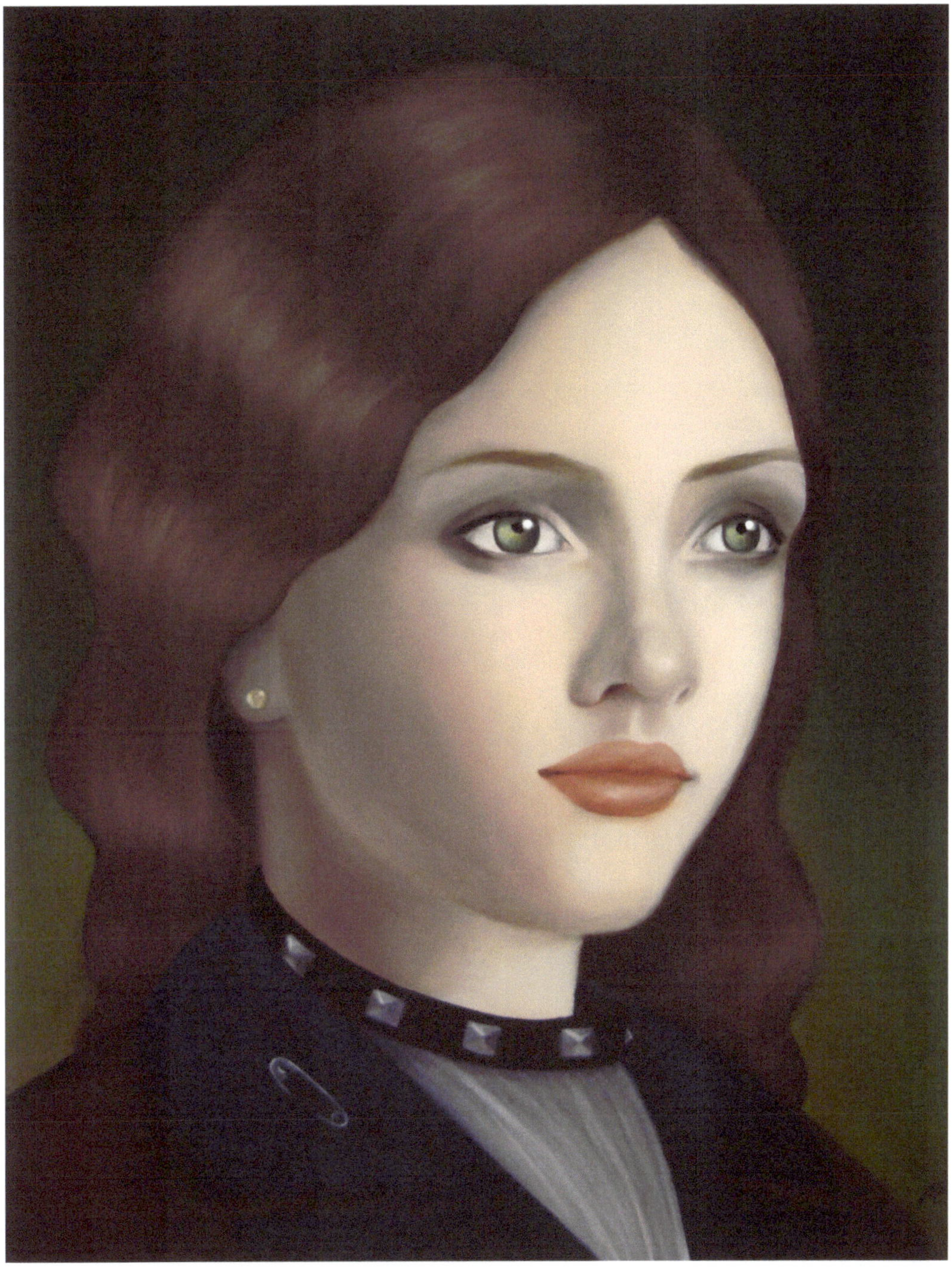

8 x 10" oil on panel

MARGARET OF VIENWRAY (1780–1846)

The illegitimate daughter of Lord Frederick bore to him by a chamber maid, it was Lord Fredericks' quick thinking that led to Margaret being raised as part of his brood. He simply placed her in the nursery with the other children. His wife and Governess had already lost count as to how many children there were - the addition went unnoticed. Although tender as a child, in time she became spoiled and extremely bored. There were four annulled marriages to various diplomats by the age of 16. With each annulment she was given a horse in hopes that riding would occupy her time instead of unsuitable men. When her marriage to the riding instructor was annulled, her father sold the horses, and gave her a parakeet instead.

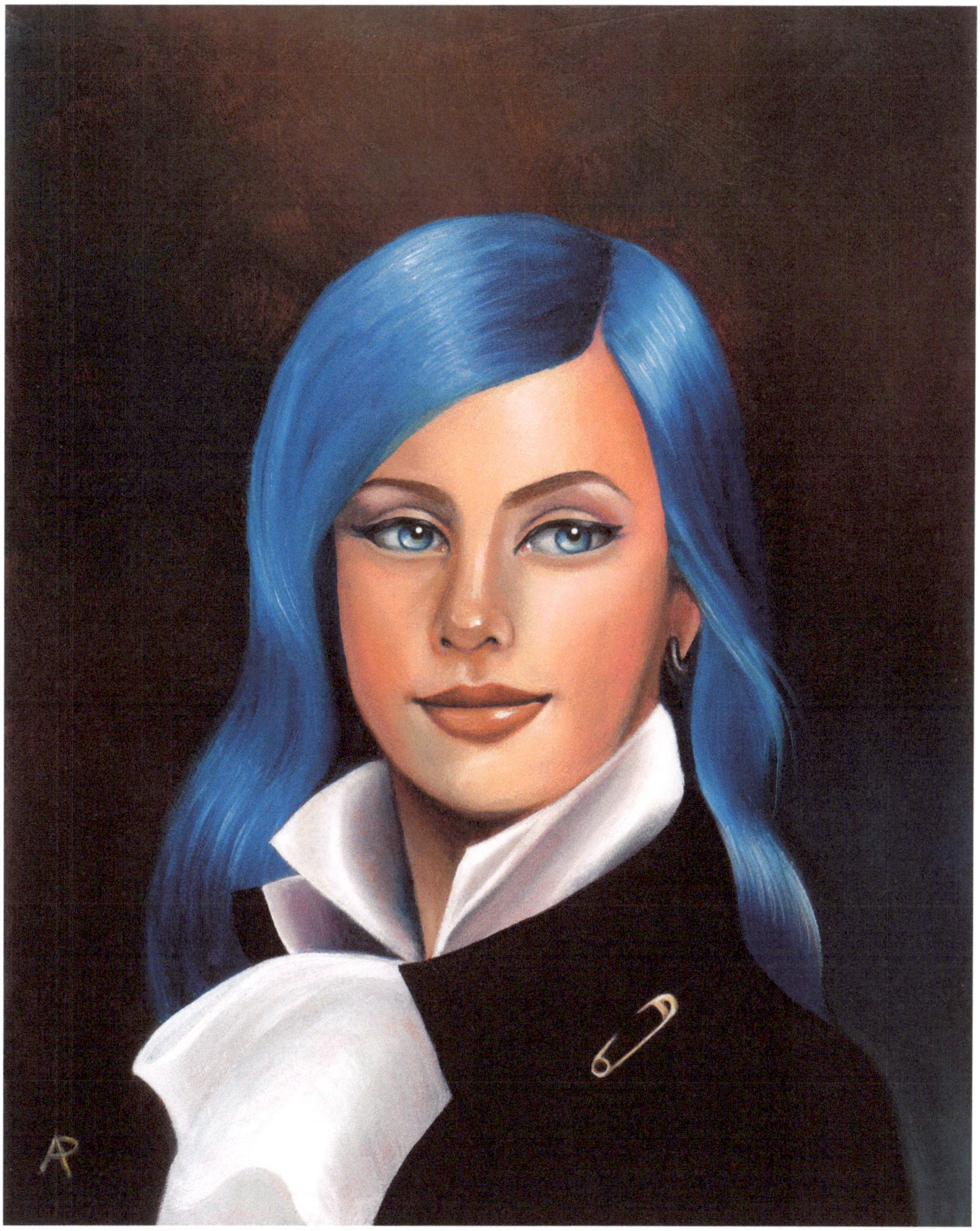

8 x 10" OIL ON PANEL

Friederica of Vienwray (1804–1874)

Born into an old aristocratic family with a predisposition for smallpox, she spent her youth being passed from one distant relative to another (each dying within a year of the next) until age 16 when she was hired by the royal court theater as an actress. She gained the Queen's favor as an amusing and attractive social weapon; when the Queen's friendship with a lady in her circle had cooled, Friederica was invited to salons and galas as a replacement, a resounding snub against anyone who had fallen out of favor. Described by men who came to pay her tribute as 'the highest creature', it is not clear if they flocked to her for her charm, her acting, or her influence with the Queen. Setting her sights on those of the most eminent condition, she retired from the stage and married the Duke of Lernigo.

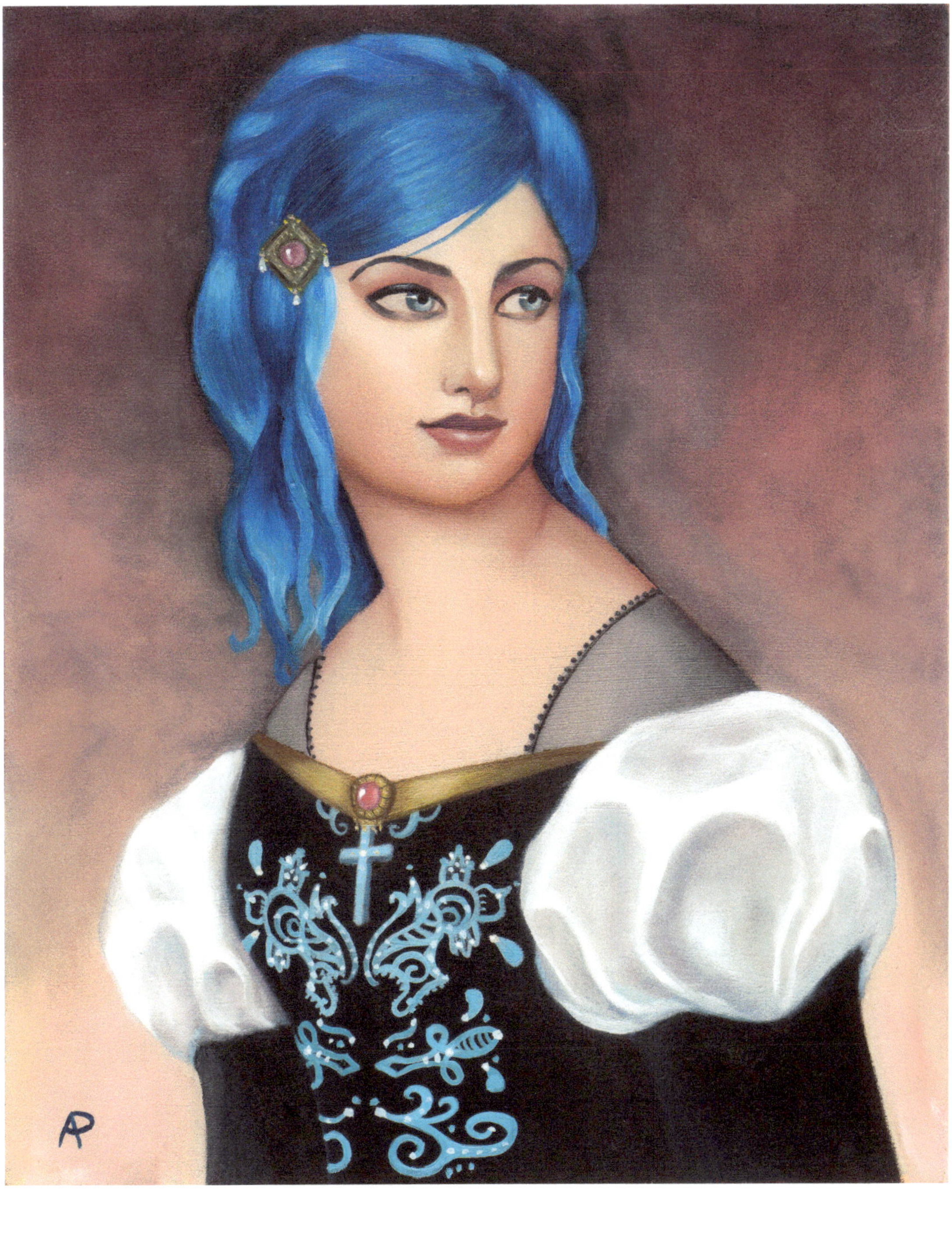

8 x 10" oil on panel

Lady Delphine of Dogole
(1596–unknown)

Charming, delicate and imaginative; she was described by her brother, a prominent Earl, as the richest and stupidest girl to ever hail from Dogole. When the nuns gave up on her convent education and sent her home, she stopped in a port town to shop and see the 'pretty ships'. It was there that she met a pirate captain; not realizing she had been kidnapped she then married him at sea and unwittingly, funded his crew for years after being told they were freedom fighters. After the death of her husband, she gained control for his fleet only to lose it in a South Pacific storm during her expedition to find Candy Apple Island. It is believed the sea chanty 'Ditzy Dame of Dogole' was inspired by her.

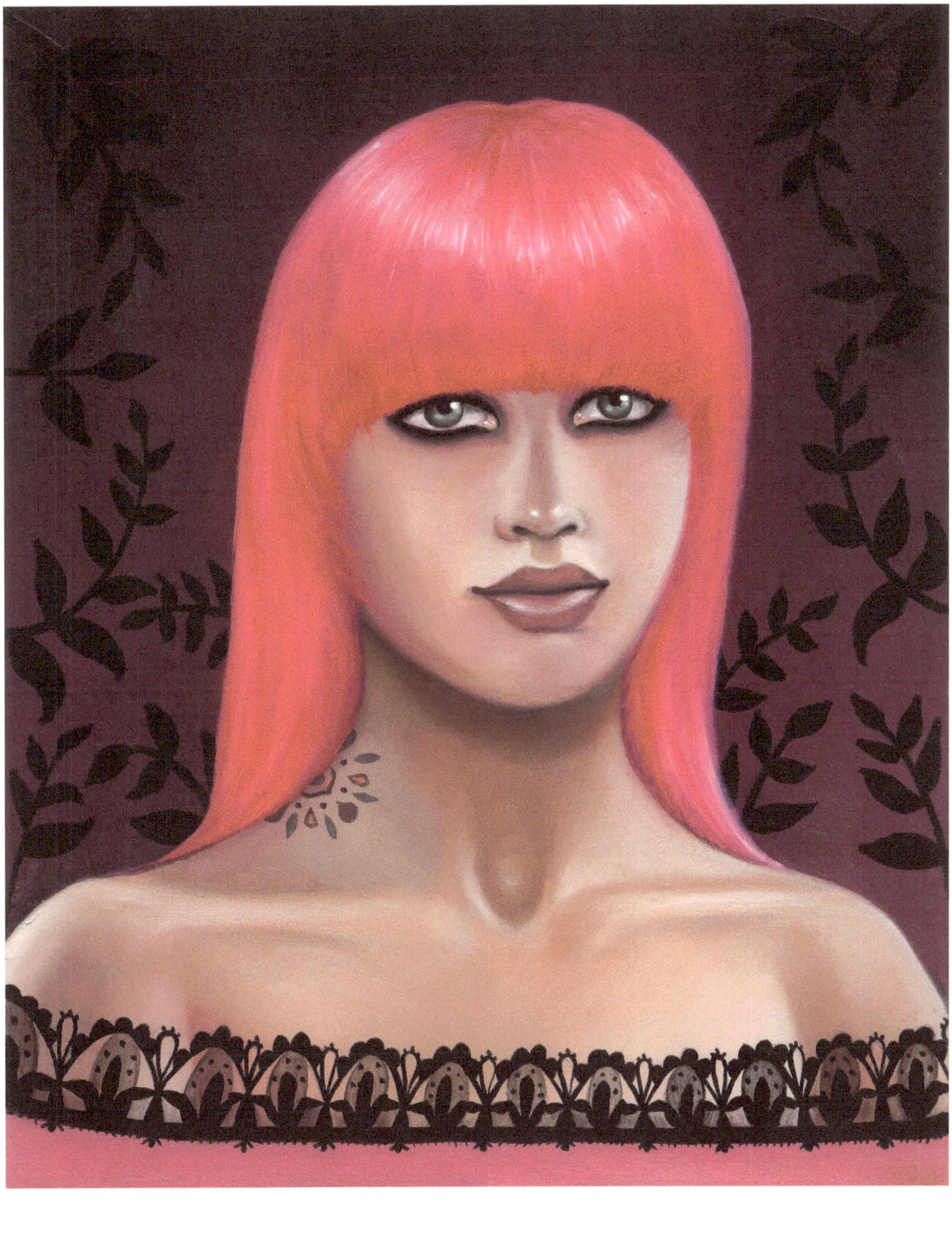

8 x 10" OIL ON PANEL

CONSTANCE (1537–1568)

The daughter of a Kessan admiral, her reputation was that of a part-time opium addict and full-time seducer of men of the cloth. It was after her investor husband suddenly collapsed and died street that an inquest was made due his secret ties with the Privy Council and the fact important papers were missing. A search throughout their town home in Kilsa revealed large amounts of bank notes, bonds and even jewels had been sewn into the canopy of her bed: gifts she had collected over the years from priests and Cardinals whom she had bedded. She later stated since she spent half her life on her back, this was the best way to secretly admire her trophies. She died of tuberculosis before fulfilling her new ambition of becoming a nun.

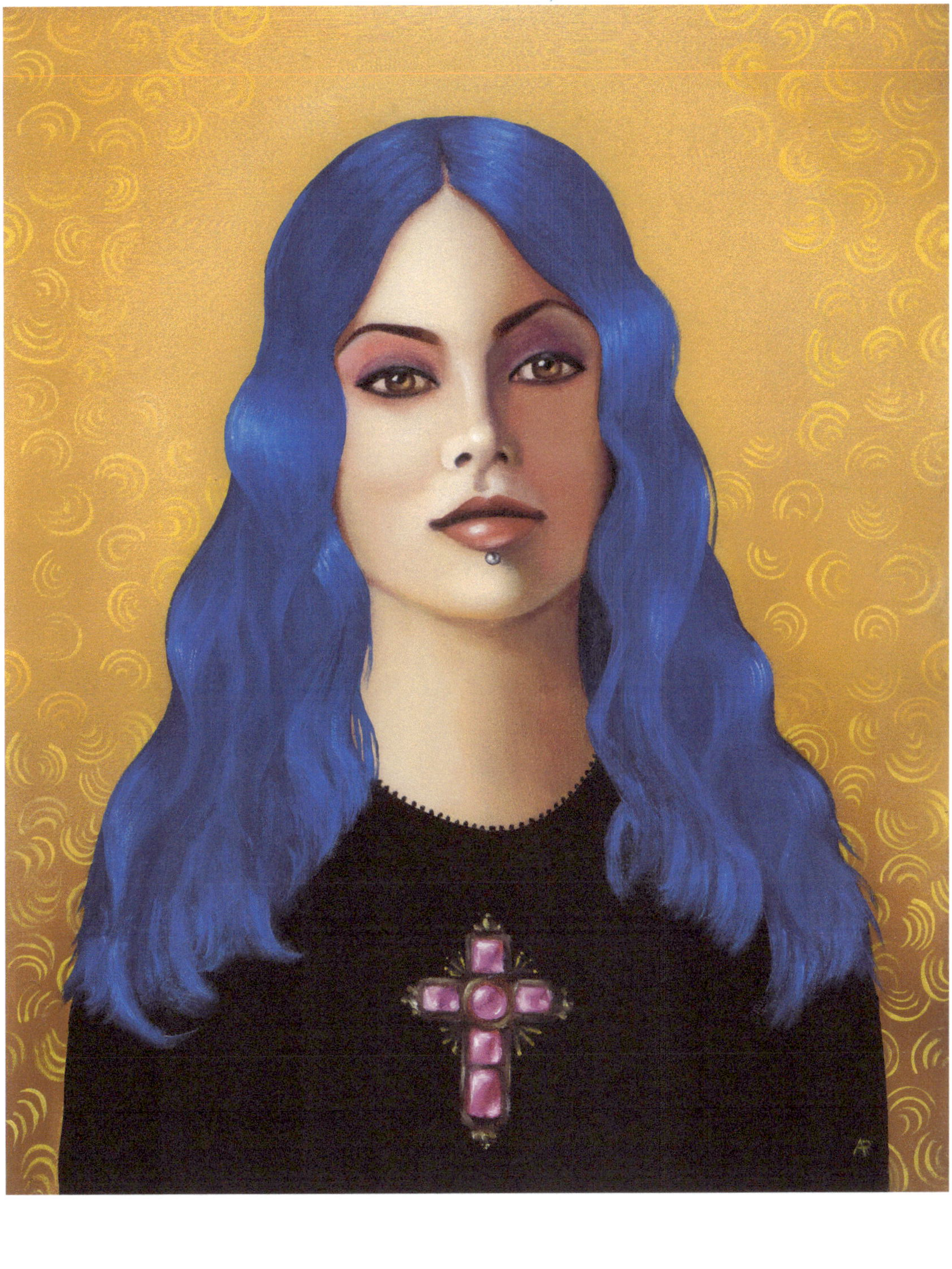

8 x 10" OIL ON PANEL

Catherine (1478–1557)

Born to a family of minor aristocrats living in poverty, her match with a well-respected judge was a happy one for several years. She had taken it in stride the day she found her husband and his valet in bed, asking for a fair divorce, and custody of their two young daughters. When he refused, she made it known that to remain married to her would become quite expensive. Her immediate string of lovers included rogues, addicts, and artists whom she offered gifts such as a rug or oil painting as they departed company. The home had become bare of furnishings and heirlooms at an alarming rate. After 7 months, the judge one evening ordered his usual wine with dinner only to be informed by the staff that all the stemware and teacups had been taken by Catherine's last visitor, his wine was thus served in a gravy boat. The judge granted the divorce shortly after.

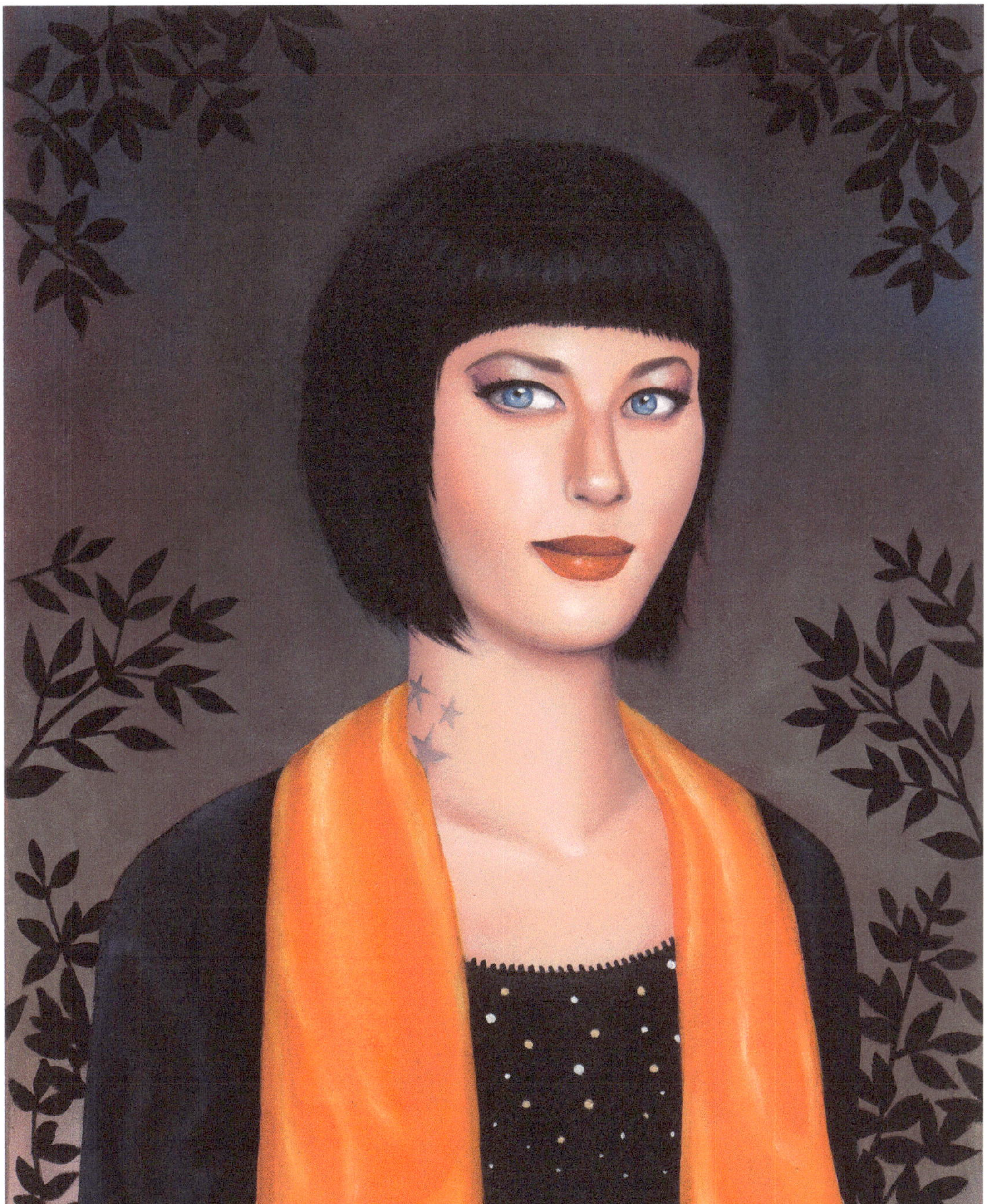

8 x 10" OIL ON PANEL

Lady Eugenia
(1588–unknown)

Daughter of a Bremmese lawyer and his stage actress mistress; she had published her first novel at age 15, thus becoming an amusement of sorts within literary circles at cafes and parties. Her short marriage to a Lord and travels to their many homes around the Continent provided the material for what would become her second novel – fortunate for the Lord he died of consumption before reading the unflattering portrait she portrayed of him. After many failed affairs with renowned writers more than half her age, she retired from writing after her 9th book, and fled to Scotland where she purchased a small cottage. She never wrote again, and instead collected stray cats

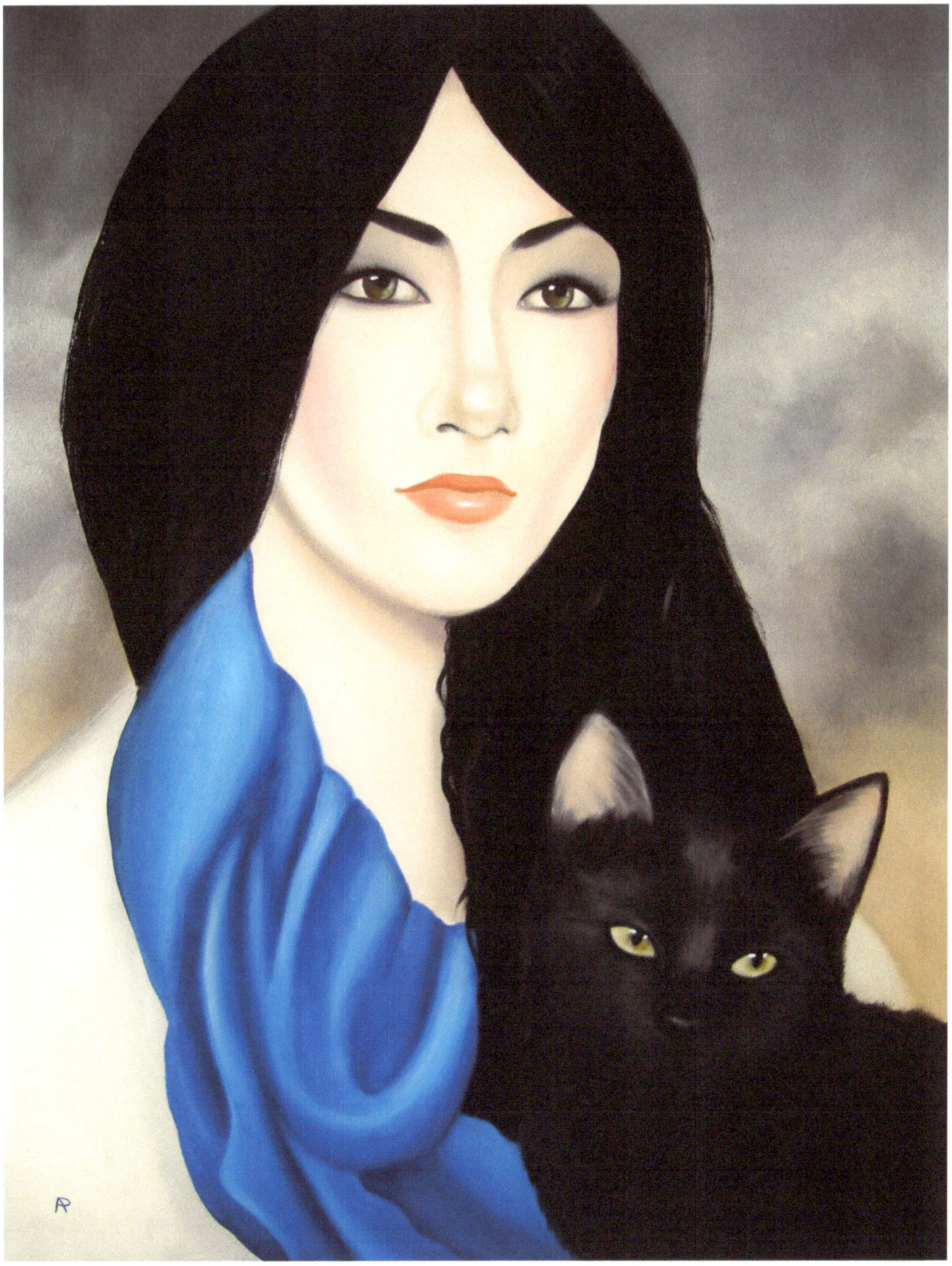

11 x 14" OIL ON PANEL

Kiki
(1680–1746)

An orphan who arrived in the capital of Kilsa at age 14, she took work as a servant for a small household, then as a delivery girl for the premier chocolatier in the city. It was the King who happened upon her as she delivered a large order for a children's party on the Palace lawn. He arranged her marriage to his favorite valet at the time. The kind old King had only good – if rather unusual – intentions in mind. After the official engagement he was to have said to Kiki, "the boy is so ugly you know, he needs a pretty girl like you to give him children that won't look like an orangutan with a lazy eye". After 7 children, none of them did.

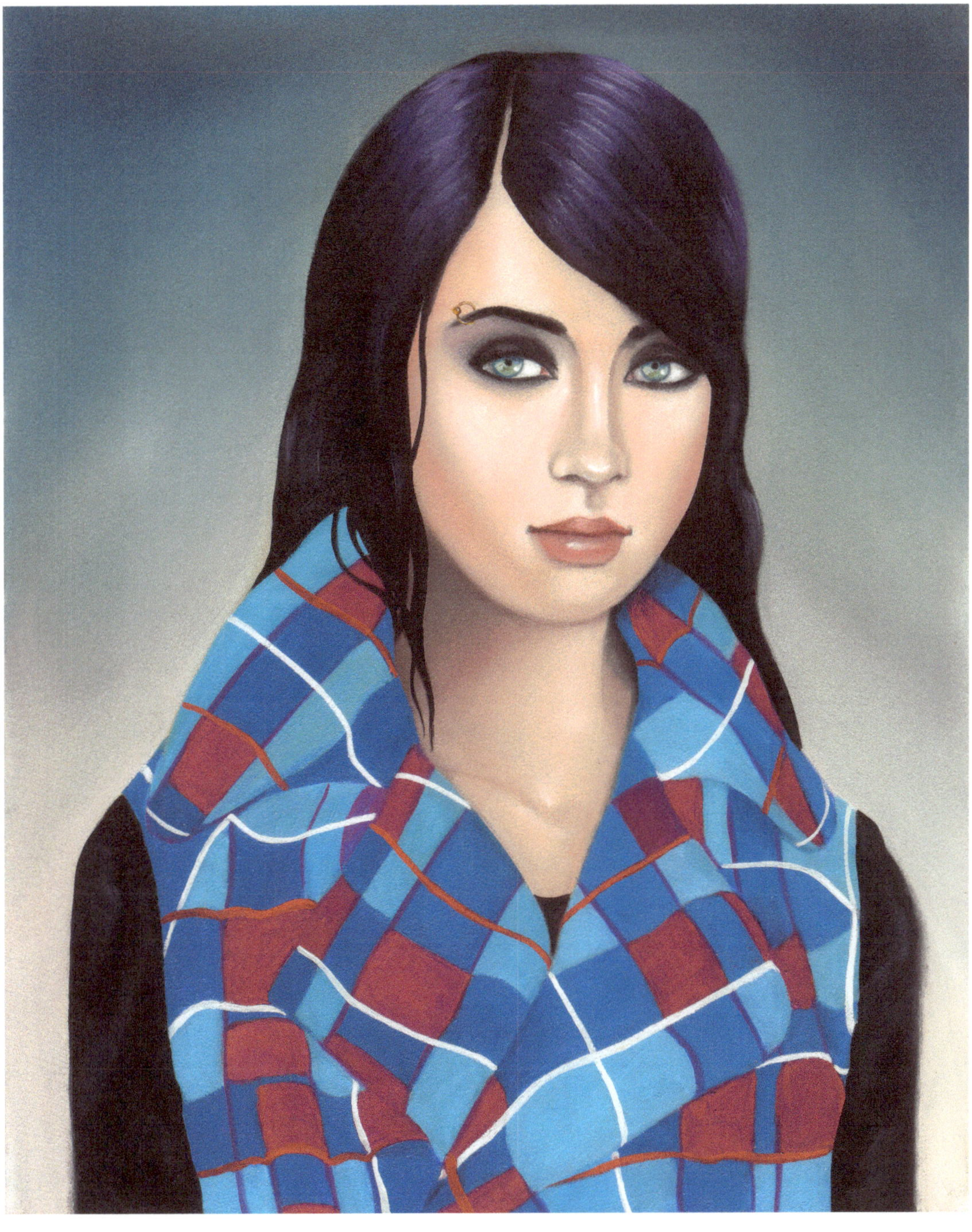

8 x 10" OIL ON PANEL

The Mirrensley Girls (1550–1600)

The daughters of a diplomat and a one-time opera singer, the girls known as Merri and Kerri spent their youth traveling from one school to another while their father was assigned to posts all over the Continent. By the time of their presentation to society, each made what was considered a good catch in the marriage market thanks to their beauty and reputation as minor celebrities, but neither lasted long. A Lord Deputy; whose dissipate lifestyle would drive Merri into the arms of his brother; and a Lieutenant Colonel who was killed in action during the Kronin Wars. With money from their father, the sisters purchased a townhouse and began a small perfume business that did quite well. Their bodies were later discovered in the attic; the door locked from the inside. One sister emaciated while the other appeared extremely obese, and each having a wound to the head. Their bizarre deaths still remain a mystery.

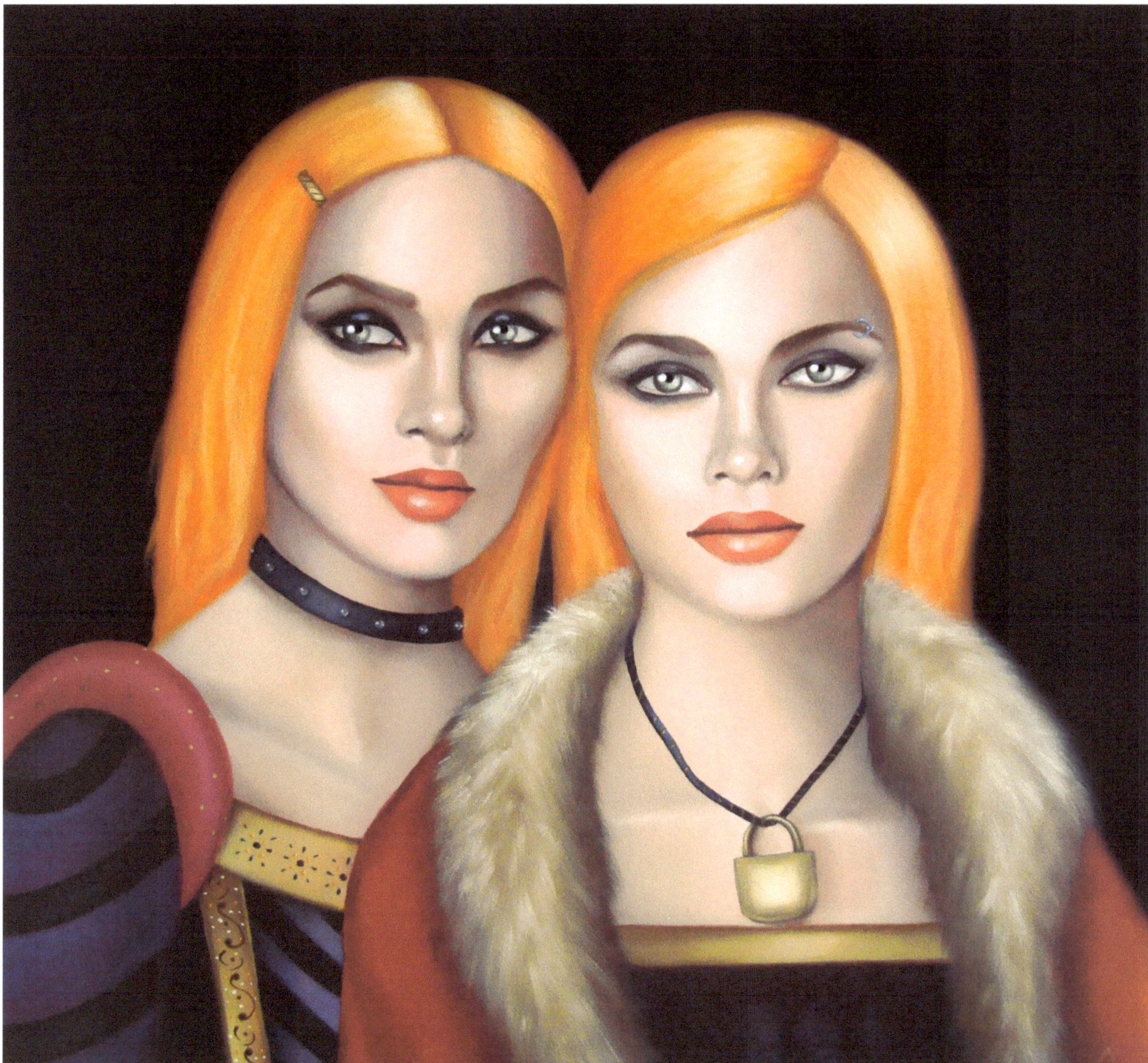

12 X 12" OIL ON PANEL

Mrs. Turner (1612–1678)

The wife of a painter's apprentice, she became the fixation and lover of many well-known artists and sculptures of her day. In fact, her derriere is said to grace many marble and bronze statues throughout the city of Kilsa – on the backsides of nymphs and goddesses – due to an extended affair with the noted sculptor Byramorri. He later conceded, "she broke my heart, and you never forget a fantastic ass like that".

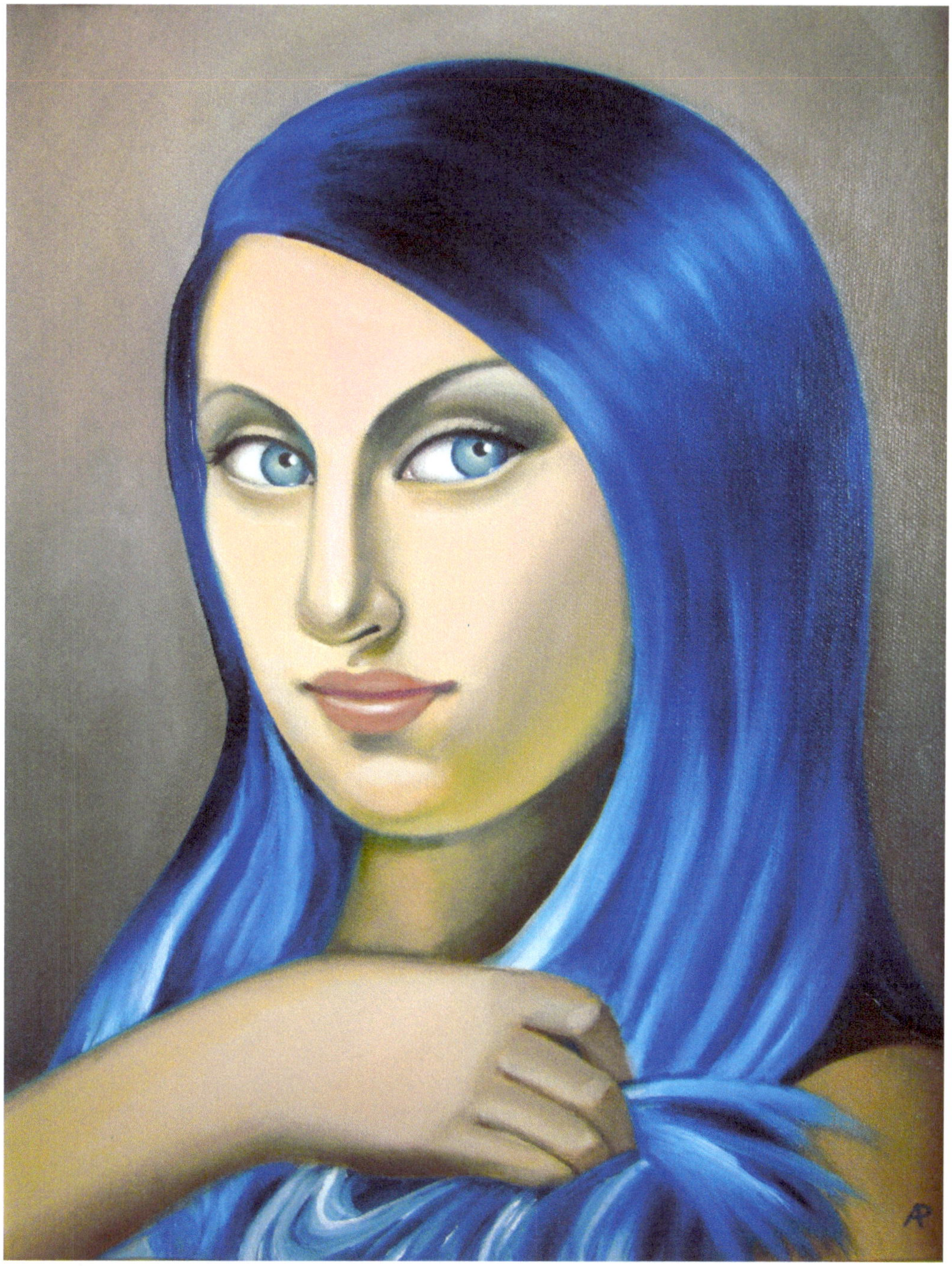

II X I4" OIL ON CANVAS

Arabella Proffer

Education

1996–00	California Institute of the Arts. Bachelor of Fine Art degree in Fine Art and Experimental Animation.

Selected Solo Exhibitions

2012	"Ephemeral Antidotes" Articulated Gallery, San Francisco, CA
2009:	"Splendor and Safety Pins" Box Heart Gallery, Pittsburgh, PA "Innocence and Arrogance" Art Whino Gallery, Washington, DC "Poise, Posture, & Profanity" William Rupnik Gallery, Cleveland, OH
2007:	"Private Empire: The National Portrait Gallery of Kessa " @ Asterisk Gallery, Cleveland, OH
2006:	"Better Living Thru Rock" Southgate House, Newport, KY "You're A Rock n' Roll Suicide" Revival, Akron, OH
2003:	"New Works" at The Ukrainian Research Institute Harvard University, Cambridge, MA
2002:	"Portraits in Punk" The Knitting Factory, Hollywood, CA
2000:	"The Last Erratic Splendor" CalArts L-Shape Gallery, Santa Clarita, CA
1996:	The Art Center Gallery, Dana Point, CA Koo's Art House, Santa Ana, CA

Selected Group Exhibitions

2011:	Gymnasia Herzlia Art Center, TelAviv, Israel "Tiny Trifecta" at The Cotton Candy Machine, Brooklyn, NY. "Notes From the Cleveland Underground" at Kunstraum Ampersand, Cologne, Germany. "Illustrious" at Wall Eye Gallery, Cleveland, OH.
2010:	Box Heart Gallery 10 Year Anniversary exhibition, Pittsburgh, PA. "Fables & Follies" Alternative Gallery, Seaside, CA. "Dark and Lovely" Parlor Gallery, Asbury Park, NJ "From Woman" group invitational, Lakeland Community College, Kirtland, OH The G40 Summit in Arlington VA, represented by Art Whino Gallery.

2009:	“Life Essentials” Art Whino Gallery represented at Art Basel Miami Beach “Feminality” Hive Gallery, Los Angeles, CA “Multiversal” Art Basel Miami Beach, FL “Warm and Fuzzy” Eclectix Gallery, El Cerrito, CA “Forgotten Saints” Congregation Gallery, Hollywood, CA “Yum Yum” CAVE Gallery, Venice, CA. “Firece Fashion” Eclectix Gallery, El Cerrito, CA “Confections” The Alternative Gallery, Seaside, CA
2008:	“All Things Cleveland” Asterisk Gallery, Cleveland, OH “Paradigm Shift” Vision Gallery, Cleveland, OH “Identity Theft” Guilford Arts Center, Guilford, CT “Ladies First” DvA Gallery, Chicago, IL “Isn’t It Romantic?” Mahan Gallery, Columbus, OH “Attack of the B Movie” Space Gallery, San Francisco, CA
2007	Collaboro show Art Whino, Alexandria, VA Artspace-Cleveland Convivium 33 Gallery, Cleveland, OH
2005	Gomi Gallery “Metal Pig at SXSW” Austin, TX ArtMetro Gallery “Small Works”, Cleveland, OH
2004	“Fashion Show” Lake Erie College Galleries, Painesville, OH “Rising Stars” Paradise Gallery, Cleveland Heights, OH “Small Works” The Muse Gallery, San Diego, CA
2003	“World Posters” East Wing Collection, London U.K. “Cannibal Flower” Hangar 1018, Los Angeles, CA “Alter Egos” Del Mar Theater, Los Angeles, CA
2002	Cannibal Flower at Spring Art Tower, Los Angeles, CA “Socially Bind” Blank Gallery, Hollywood, CA
2001	“Blood Moon” Headquarters Gallery (curator). Hollywood, CA Basswerks Gallery “Dust Moths & Cobwebs” Los Angeles, CA
1999	“The Toy Show” CalArts D102 Gallery, Santa Clarita, CA. “The Organic Show” CalArts Lime Gallery, Santa Clarita, CA
1998	Barnsdall Art Center, “All City” Hollywood, CA
1997	“The Foundation” CalArts Main Gallery, Santa Clarita, CA Sotheby’s Artlink Auction, Tel Aviv, Israel
1996	The Moscow Pen Club “25 years of Ardis” Moscow, Russia

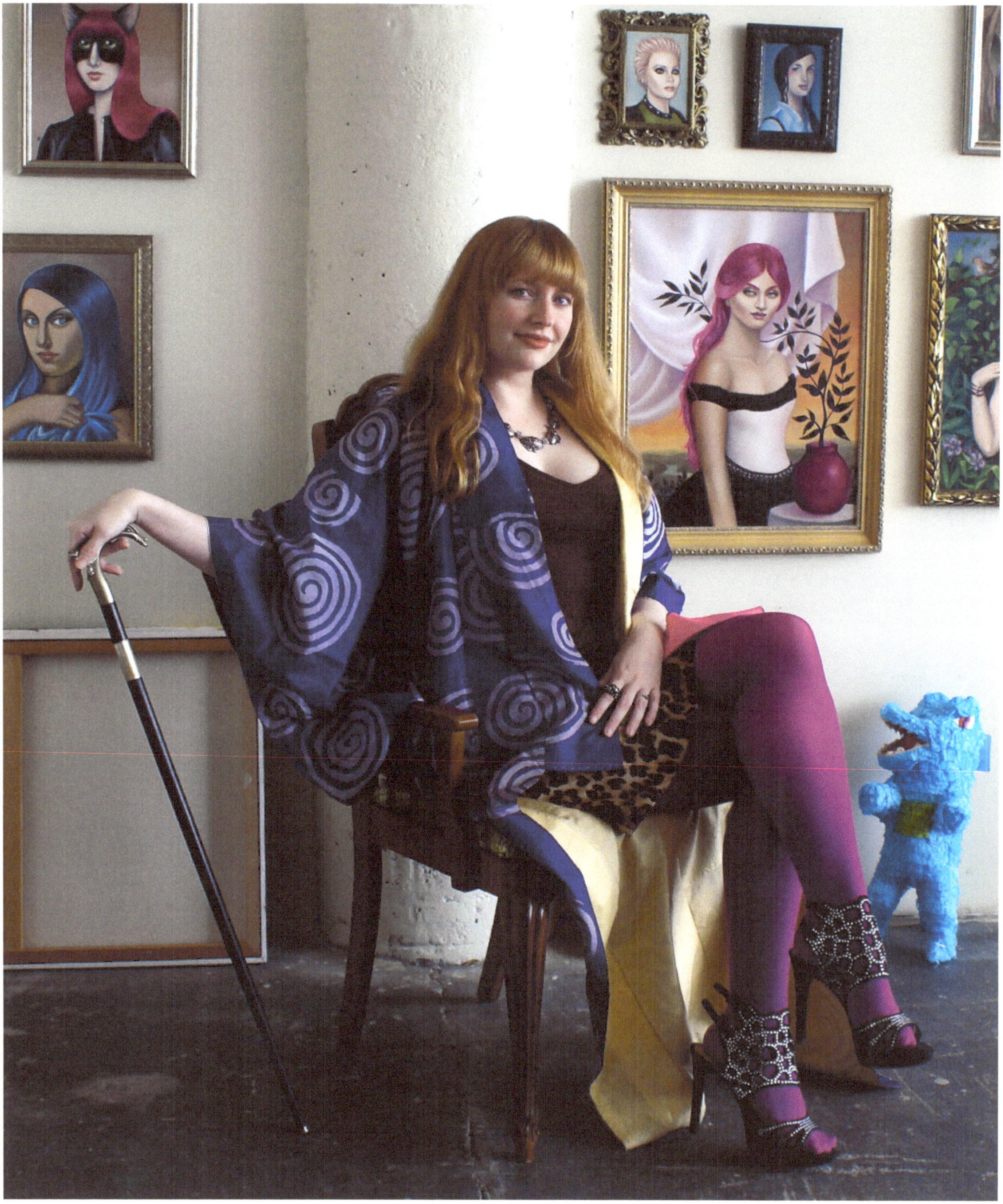

Cooperative Press

partners in publishing

Cooperative Press was founded in 2007 by Shannon Okey, a voracious reader as well as writer and editor, who had been doing freelance acquisitions work, introducing authors with projects she believed in to editors at various publishers.

Although working with traditional publishers can be very rewarding, there are some books that fly under their radar. They're too avant-garde, or the marketing department doesn't know how to sell them, or they don't think they'll sell 50,000 copies in a year.

5,000 or 50,000. Does the book matter to that 5,000? Then it should be published.

In 2009, Cooperative Press changed its named to reflect the relationships we have developed with authors working on books. We work together to put out the best quality books we can and share in the proceeds accordingly.

Thank you for supporting independent publishers and authors.

COOPERATIVEPRESS.COM

AT LEFT: PROFFER IN HER STUDIO

www.ingramcontent.com/pod-product-compliance
Ingram Content Group UK Ltd.
Pitfield, Milton Keynes, MK11 3LW, UK
UKHW061032310726
14089UKWH00009B/206
* 9 7 8 1 9 3 7 5 1 3 0 2 3 *